Real Men or Real Teachers?

Contradictions in the Lives of Men Elementary School Teachers

Paul Sargent, Ph.D.

Department of Sociology
San Diego State University

Men's Studies Press
Harriman, Tennessee 37748

Men's Studies Press, Harriman, Tennessee 37748
Copyright 2001 by the Men's Studies Press.

Robert L. Anderson's poem "No One Told Me" is reprinted by permission. Copyright 1991 by Yevrah Ornstein (Ed.), *From the hearts of men* (pp. 60-61). New York: Fawcett.

Cover and text design by Sally Ham Govan
Cover photo: Digital Imagery © 2001 PhotoDisc, Inc.

First Edition
ISBN: 0-9671794-3-2

Library of Congress Cataloging-in-Publication Data

Sargent, Paul, 1946-
    Real Men or Real Teachers? : contradictions in the lives of men elementary school teachers / Paul Sargent.—1st ed.
        p.cm.
    Includes bibliographical references and indexes.
    ISBN 0-9671794-3-2 (pbk. : alk. paper)
    1. Male elementary school teachers—United States. 2. Male elementary school teachers—United States-Attitudes. 3. Sex differences in education—United States. I.
    Title: Contradictions in the lives of men elementary school teachers. II. Title.

LB1776.2.S27 2001
372.11'0081'0973—dc21
                                00-049552

Dedication

For Martha, my friend and partner, whose unfailing confidence in me helped me through innumerable bouts of self-doubt.

Contents

Acknowledgements

Thanks to Mike Messner for his capable guidance and immense patience as my mentor and friend. Mostly, I thank him for his unwavering support throughout the entire process of graduate school and this study.

My thanks, too, to Jim Doyle of the Men's Studies Press for his enthusiasm and the incredible time and energy he has devoted to this work. I am also indebted to the many reviewers who have helped to make this a more accessible and lively work.

Finally, I can't begin to adequately thank the wonderful men who gave up their precious time and opened up their lives to me during the interviews. I can only hope that they feel the publication of this work, in some small way, compensates them for everything they have done for all of us.

Preface

    This study is about the lives of a group of men who teach in the primary grades. I believe these stories will be as intriguing and engaging for others as they were for me. Other men teachers,[1] other men, other feminists, and other sociologists may all appreciate the disclosures of these men. My intended audience is none of these groups, however. In *The Ethnographic Interview*, James Spradley tells us that a wise publisher recommends we write for a specific person and then many others will likely want to read what we've created.[2] I have written this specifically for the many men who would be wonderful teachers, parents, or caregivers but have experienced negative sanctions whenever they have attempted to lead gender-atypical lives. I believe we have paid too little attention to the societal forces that work to ensure that our young men become competitive, success-oriented, independent, and stoic rather than warm, nurturing, and open, as they are capable of becoming. A secondary audience whom I've kept in mind is the researcher who is considering an inquiry into the lives of men, *as men*. I hope that after reading this, researchers will examine closely the pre-conceived notions about men that can so easily and unintentionally be brought to bear on the research process.

    These are stories from the heart and, while there are important policy implications in these narratives and the subsequent interpretations, there is much more. Here is an opportunity to connect to the real life experiences and feelings of a group of men who in many ways do not fit the traditional definitions of masculinity. They not only live lives removed from the usual meaning of masculine success; their interpersonal styles often defy the typical image of stoic, distant, and non-disclosing that we tend to attach to men. Instead, they are warm, open, sharing, and wonderful to be with. While most are enamored with teaching, they express some disappointment and not a little anxiety over the issues I examine here.

In reading other researchers' monographs, I notice that many describe how they chose their projects. In particular, they often describe the way a sociological question drove them early on to pursue the collection and analysis of data ever more vigorously. I must confess that initially there was no such question for me, at least not one that I could articulate in frank sociological terms. The project actually took hold of me, not vice versa. There was, from the beginning, a haunting sense that important ideas and feelings were hiding just below the surface of seemingly commonplace happenings. The emerging data and further questions and puzzles that these data generated were what drove this study, not some over-arching theory that needed to be tested. It was only when trying to assemble the ideas I'd collected that I realized I was seeing the emergence of new theory, or at least a new application of theory. It isn't entirely clear to me at what point in the project I identified enough of a pattern to compare it to any perspective with which I was familiar. Prior to this project, I certainly couldn't lay claim to "practicing" my sociology or my feminism from any given perspective. Even now, as I explain in this work, the perspective on which I rest is a hybrid of previously existing ones.

My involvement in this study accomplished at least three things: it revealed insights into some lives that had previously remained hidden; it demonstrated, for me, a way of applying powerful theories about women to the lives of men; and it confirmed for me that I am a sociologist and a feminist. Although I had proclaimed both of the latter on many occasions, I always felt my claims could be quite easily challenged and not nearly as easily defended. I no longer feel that is true.

I found myself with a dual task: to find out what was really happening in men's lives while simultaneously trying to determine the best way to discover this. Standard deductive research didn't appeal to me and seemed antithetical to getting close to these men. I anticipated that "getting close," in and of itself, would become an additional task since the teachers and I likely grew up with the same homophobic mandates that work to keep men apart from each other.

It occurred to me that if I was successful in completing this project, I could contribute to several areas of knowledge simultaneously including knowledge about the structure and practices of a predominately female occupation and how these contribute to maintaining the occupation as women's work; knowledge about a group of men who voluntarily put themselves in a marginalized position compared to hegemonic masculinity; and knowledge about how to break down barriers and do interpretive, close, personal research with and for men.

The issues that arose from my conversations with the men in my study eventually linked with interviews I undertook with men enrolled in colleges of education. These later interviews were suggested by the men teachers' comments describing their experiences in teacher training. In addition, all of these conversations began to resonate with journals and papers that had been submitted by the students in my gender classes over the last six years. The major course requirement for the class is to work with the children in the campus children's center and submit an ethnographic paper based on these experiences.

I invite my readers to listen carefully to what these men are telling us. Woven into the stories on the following pages are clear indicators of how vigorously an institution can work to instill gender into its members. On a more optimistic note, there are also clear indicators of ways we can work to disassemble this system. What is especially important is that in these stories it is *men* who are encountering obstacles to "crossing over" into gender-atypical realms. How willing are we, as a society, to recognize these impediments as real and to lend a hand?

What I present in this book is a hard copy version that roughly resembles my internal discourse. This means it contains many digressions, U-turns, musings, and unresolved dilemmas, rather than being a clean, linear presentation. To quote Mary Wollstonecraft:

> When the ideas, and matters of fact, are once taken
> in, they lie by for use, till some fortuitous circum-
> stances make the information dart into the mind

with illustrative force, that has been received at very different periods of our lives. Like the lightning's flash are many recollections; one idea assimilating and explaining another, with astonishing rapidity.... Over those instantaneous associations we have little power; for when the mind is once enlarged by excursive flights, or profound reflections, the raw materials will, in some degree, arrange themselves.[3]

Like Wollstonecraft two hundred years ago, I make only a little apology for this transgression while at the same time inviting the reader to recognize the process as distinctly human.

~ 1 ~

The Project That Wouldn't Go Away

"I think you can change things that way. Mostly that is the way things are changed, by writing about them."

—Doc in *Street Corner Society*[1]

"No Other Men!"

"No other men!" Three simple words glared out at me from the first page of the little notebook that I had put into service for my research into the lives of men elementary teachers. I wrote this statement as I waited in the tiny, cluttered, very busy office of a local elementary school for the first of thirty-five interviews with men who teach in the early grades (K-3). Like most field researchers, I had gotten into the habit of jotting down key words that I could later expand into richer, more detail-filled narratives in my journal.

My observations that day began as soon as I stepped out of my car and began walking across the parking lot toward the school buildings. On most days, I rather enjoy that my old VW Bug tends to attract attention, but that day was different. I felt as though I, and not the car, was painted bright orange. I had arrived at the end of the school day, and the place was a beehive of activity. Everywhere I looked, small bodies were being ushered into cars or buses, to another location, or simply being tended to as they waited for their transportation home. All of the ushers and tenders were women. In fact, every adult in sight was a woman, including the bus drivers and the drivers of the cars queued up in the street.

This image would continue, with some small deviations, until the last day of interviewing—no other men besides the teacher I interviewed, the occasional custodian, and myself. Other men were on the sites, of course. Nationally, about fifteen percent of the personnel of elementary schools are men, including teachers, principals, and support staff.[2] I simply did not happen to encounter them during my visits and, according to many of the men I spoke with, like Ben,[3] the teachers often make the same observation I had in their own mental "notebooks."

> Ben: Yeah, I'm the only guy on this site ... besides
> the custodian. I was the only man at my last site,
> too.

Throughout my project I was continually amazed at the absence of men in the environment. It is one thing to read about an occupation being gendered, but it is an entirely different thing to see it first hand. My past experiences in public safety had provided me with considerable contact with jobs where men *or* women predominate, but none of the occupations with which I was familiar (police, fire-fighting, nursing) was as obviously gendered as primary teaching.

Another type of entry that appeared on the first and many subsequent pages was an acknowledgment of the ease with which images from my own life began to emerge. Personal reflection in qualitative work is, unlike in more traditional positivist approaches, an important part of how we, as researchers, make sense of our research experience. Since we are the research instrument, keeping tabs on what is happening to our internal conversation regarding data, analysis, and our own feelings is important. For example, the following excerpt from my journal shows how much just being on the elementary school grounds affected me:

Through the window I can see the walls decorated with children's projects. The theme is clearly "autumn" because each sheet has a yellow, red, or brown leaf carefully colored with crayon. I remember bringing real leaves to school so that we could paste them on construction paper. I can almost smell the paste.

There is apparently nothing unusual about the past resurfacing in the face of revisiting schoolyards. This was a common occurrence according to teachers such as Howard and Barry.

Howard: Probably one of the most common reactions I get when I tell people I'm a teacher is, "Oh, I remember those days," or "I still remember what my fifth grade (or whatever) teacher used to say."

*****

Barry: Every time we have parent night I have several of them tell me how just coming to the school brings back so many memories. I think most people only remember the good things about elementary school.

I had only one man teacher in elementary school. My most vivid memory of him was when I saw him marching in a parade in his starched, white Navy Reserve officer's uniform. It's odd that my clearest memory of him is in war garb. I can conjure up a few other images of him bringing science projects for us to work on and students from other classes would come into our room just to join in the task of planting bean seeds, making barometers and periscopes, or magnetizing everything on which we could get our hands.

When I catch mental glimpses of the other teachers, all women, I see them doing many other things. They are talking, gesturing, writing, and moving about the room in myriad activities. I remember, too, as a child, this odd kind of familiarity that the women teachers seemed to have, this unquestioned right that they had to touch me, talk to me, get close to me, and ask me personal questions. As a child I seemed to sense, through these women's touch and words, a strange connection between home and school.

As a parent of four elementary school age children I noticed the same kind of familiarity, this kind of touching and "fussing" that mark a difference between the ways mothers are presented tending to children in our society and the ways fathers are. I also noticed that there was an attempted connection between the teachers and my wife, rather than with me, in spite of my being the one at home most of the time and the person who most often made contact with the teachers. Even my own children's insistence that "my dad takes care of that" did not deter them from sending notes, requests, and instructions home to "Mom." When I volunteered to be the class "parent" one year, the teacher concluded she would have two of us—a class mom and a class "Mr. Mom." Her explanation was that there were things that she "needed a mom to do." This was said in that manner that people use when they're telling us something we should know and therefore do not need explained. What I did not recognize then, but see clearly now, is that these behaviors are symptoms of how gendered the culture of teaching really is.

Beyond the demographics alluded to above, there are deeper issues regarding the ways that gendered workplaces are organized. In the world of elementary teaching, the assumption is that all the adults who attend to the needs of the children (the "typical actors" in this particular social scene) are women. This is far more than an issue of numbers. We are so accustomed to seeing either women or men performing certain tasks that we assume these tasks must require some essential, requisite talent that is sex-specific.[4] Saying "women *or* men" contributes to the problem by reinforcing the notion that there are two mutually exclusive categories and we each must fit into only one of them and this model likely conjures up essential biological, rather than constructed cultural, groupings.

Gender is a "social construction," a concept manufactured through human interaction but often treated as "natural" by those who created it. The example I use with my students is the clock on the classroom wall. The hours, minutes, and seconds that seemingly rule our lives are artifacts, products of human thinking, yet we speak of them and integrate them into our lives as though we had discovered them in nature and employed them for our use. In most recent academic writings, sex and gender have been separated as having biological and cultural roots, respectively. Gender is constructed when, knowing only another person's biological sex, we mistakenly feel confident enough to make assumptions about the person's abilities and limitations and to hold expectations for them. If we conceptualize gender in this way it allows us to (1) recognize that gender is constructed and reconstructed regularly, (2) be free of concepts that define gender as some kind of fixed essence, (3) appreciate that gender is fluid and may be constructed differently in different situations, and (4) understand that there can be multiple femininities and masculinities present at any given historical moment. As Robert Connell has argued, these multiple masculinities and femininities will be hierarchically aligned so as to produce a "hegemonic" form of masculinity and an "emphasized" type of femininity.[5] This constructionist model also allows us to include the important issue of power in our analysis of gender so that we can see that, in a given interaction, the inequality of power between participants allows one definition of the situation (and of gender) to be privileged over another. Finally, we can conceptualize these genders as relational. The multiple masculinities and femininities are intertwined into a complex system in ways that have not yet been entirely unraveled. They are interconnected and mutually interdependent for existence and meaning. Changes in one aspect of the "sex/gender system" will precipitate changes in other areas.[6] These resultant effects are often unanticipated and may very well go unnoticed except to those whose lives are directly affected. Unless those experiencing these effects are given voice to express their distress, we are unlikely ever to know about them.

Like Connell, I find it most valuable to see gender as a social construction and focus on the way people create gender on a day-to-day basis. In addition, I am a devout believer in the "Thomas Theorem" that simply tells us that people's own beliefs about what is true are the source of their decisions regarding action.[7] It is there-fore instructive to ascertain what it is that people believe to be true. One of the primary goals of qualitative research, and one of the defining differences between it and more traditional, quantitative methodology, is the search for people's underlying beliefs about the world and how it works. People's beliefs have a source, and often that source is the stated beliefs and explicit behaviors of others. Other times the source is found in the institutionalized practices and ideologies that we are immersed in at various moments.[8] In other words, the "rules" that are in play, often implicitly, in any given instance, influence our decisions regarding how to behave and how to feel (or at least how to express feelings).

Connell's perspective is that gendered behavior is created and maintained through the interaction of the social division of labor (which jobs are assigned to whom), the dispersion of power (which groups' ideas prevail), and the distribution of cathexis. While men, in general, are unquestionably privileged in the first two, we may actually be debilitated in the third. Cathexis, in its broadest meaning, refers to the access one has to ways of fulfilling one's emotional needs, and the literature is replete with evidence affirming men's emotional constipation. By examining the positions of persons in relation to their access to these three resources, we can envision a social matrix that produces multiple masculinities and femininities simultaneously. The prevailing (hegemonic) masculinity as we move into the twenty-first century is white, heterosexual, able-bod-ied, upper middle-class, thirty-something, stoic, and Protestant, or what Audre Lorde has labeled the "mythical norm" to which we all are subject to comparison.[9]

Perhaps the best way to think about gender is as a "perform-ance," or something we "do" rather than something we "are."[10] Of course, we are strongly encouraged to "do" our gender correctly or else face having our "character, motives, and predispositions" called into question.[11] In this way, we tend to hold individuals accountable rather than calling attention to the weaknesses or fallacies of the gender order itself. Once again, the effect is to produce the impres-sion that gender categories are "natural." This leads to one's performance as a member of a category being open to evaluation and to being compared to the "standard," thus producing a powerful mechanism of social control. One of the key objectives of feminist activism is to reveal these mechanisms of social control for what they are and to expose the way we have constructed gender as "natural" and composed of two mutually exclusive categories. The perpetuation of the gender binary, or system of gender relations, indeed depends on the maintenance of two gender categories. Each is enforced and reinforced by a set of mutually interdependent institutional practices, ideologies, and social control mechanisms. The destabilization, deconstruction, or disassembling of the sex/gender system has to progress at both the institutional (organizational) and interactional (interpersonal) levels and be focused on both "sides" of the gender divide that these phenomena produce and reproduce. That is, we must call into question the legitimacy of *both* the femininities *and* the masculinities produced and the multiple ways these interact.

As Robert Connell has suggested, perhaps the place for us to look for opportunities to disassemble the gender order is at sites where gender is coming under strain.[12] One such site is the gendered workplace, particularly those occupations in which we find women or men engaged in activities not seen as typical of their sex. By looking carefully at the kinds of interactions that are present within these areas of strain, we are likely to discover that the "normal" rules of interaction are not in place (or at least they aren't of much use to the participants). Women who enter "men's" work and men who enter "women's" work may be at "ground zero" of a potential chain reaction of change in the gender order, and the consequence of their presence may produce artifacts that we can read and thus gain insights into gender that were previously hidden from us. This is one of the ideas that brought me to this research.

As I pursued this project, I found myself analyzing my own life as much as, if not more than, the lives of the men with whom I was speaking. I remember how excited I was in junior high school when we got to pick a musical instrument to learn. We could actually take one home and not return it until the end of the school year. I chose a violin. It was my first choice, and I was delighted that one was still available when, proceeding alphabetically, the teacher called my name. This all happened before lunch, and by the end of the school day it seemed as though every kid I knew, girls and boys, had heard that I'd chosen the violin and commented on my "sissy" choice. I tried unsuccessfully to carry the easily recognizable case home in a manner that would prevent identification. On my arrival home, my mother continued on from where my schoolmates had left off by comparing me to Liberace, a popular musician who delighted in exaggerating effeminate behavior. The next day I returned the violin and picked up an old, battered baritone horn. As an adult, I've told myself I should have been stronger, should have stood up for what I valued, but like most twelve-year-olds, what I valued most was fitting in, being normal, not being ridiculed. Perhaps that event partially explains why I feel it is imperative to identify the events in men's lives that influence them away from the activities identified as feminine. It may also explain my aversion to notions of the "fragile male ego" as a source of the choices men make. This overused phrase is often invoked to explain, disparagingly, why men may make the decision to act in stereotypical ways. Such an explanation seems too facile, too tautological. It ignores the powerful cultural messages that surround and influence us.

My relationship with feminism has been a rocky road. In the early 1970s, I enrolled in a college course with the title "Women and Men in Contemporary Society." The course was canceled prior to the first meeting, but I had received a copy of the outline and reading list. A major requirement for the course was to write a critical review of one of the works listed, one of which was Mary Shelley's *Frankenstein*. With great curiosity, I read the novel and came away with a strong sense that there was something disturbing about reading a work that touched my personal self so closely yet was written by a woman, and one who had lived so long ago. Having been recently released from military service, I felt a strange connection with Shelley's creature for, like him, I and other soldiers had been "created" for a particular purpose—war. Like the creature, many of us had a powerful feeling that we were suddenly repulsive to look at.

In the following passage, the creature admonishes Dr. Frankenstein, his creator:

> I am malicious because I am miserable. Am I not shunned and hated by all mankind? You, my creator, would tear me to pieces and triumph; remember that and tell me why I should pity man more than he pities me? [13]

In reading some of Shelley's short stories, I found Shelley often alluded to the softer side of men, a hidden side that emerged, breaking through a tough outer shell, only in the most special of circumstances.[14] She seemed to have a perceptiveness about the hearts of men that I found refreshing. It was while I was looking for biographical information about Mary Shelley that I discovered the writings of her mother, Mary Wollstonecraft. Her insights into the ways that different educations and socializations create existing gender differences is still, I believe, the quintessential model of what is now "liberal feminism." Liberal feminists believe that if men and women are allowed equal access to educational and occupational opportunities, both will live more meaningful and personally fulfilling lives.[15]

I will probably never know what kind of critique would have ultimately come out of my attendance in the course. I do know, however, that Wollstonecraft's eloquent statements about the condition of women opened my mind to a radical vision of society. In addition, I found that I was questioning the gender roles of *both* men and women, questions that had not previously occurred to me to be reasonable since most of the discourse at the time focused on the condition of women.

Most studies of crossing over into gender-atypical occupations are centered on the experiences of women working in male-dominated work environments. By looking at, and listening to stories about, the lives of women working in men's worlds we can see clearly the ways in which the societal division of labor contributes to the subordination of women. For example, Susan Martin published a groundbreaking work describing her findings about the lives of women who crossed over into the masculine world of police work.

> The entry of female officers threatens to disrupt both the prevalent norms and the group solidarity of the policemen. Physical differences between the sexes become a central focus of concern. Underlying the arguments about women's physical characteristics, however, is the men's fear that women will fail to uphold the norms of policing, thus making their work more difficult and dangerous, and less rewarding. Yet they also fear that if women do fulfill the norms, the meanings of masculinity and femininity become blurred.[16]

In her summary statement, Martin has expressed several of the issues that typically arise from studies of women entering "men's work," and they explain why these inquiries are so important to a general mission of disassembling gender. What reasons can be given for studying the lives of men working in women's occupations? For one thing, we need to spend more time studying men *as men* to understand who we are apart from the political and economic statuses we occupy. In particular, we need to pay more attention to how we feel about our experiences as men. We need a study of men's experiences as men, rather than more inquiries into the statuses that men hold, projects that leave men's lives unexamined. Men's own experiences must be seen as important in themselves. An important part of "an accurate study of men and masculinity," as Jeff Hearn argues, "is an appreciation of the positive features of men's lived experiences." He suggests we can use life-course studies to ascertain how the gender order affects men's lives.[17] We may discover how as men we understand our feelings and ourselves in terms of our interaction with existing social categories. This leads us into concrete studies of men's subjective experiences, just as, according to Harry Brod, women's studies have led us to "establish the objectivity of women's experiences and thereby validate the legitimacy of women's experiences."[18] In this way, we are able to address many of the same goals as women's studies, however different the particulars on which we focus.

Second, by studying masculinity and extending the women's studies debates to men's studies, we would add to our growing knowledge of the sex/gender system as a whole. Harriett Bradley has suggested that we need to extend women's studies to an understanding of how the experiences of *both* women and men are linked *via* the sex/gender system.[19] Extension of women's studies into men's lives will require a "sustained, systematically focused study of masculinities," rather than the more fragmented insights that come from women's studies' critiques of patriarchy.[20] Focused studies into men's lives can help us to uncover and understand men's unique experiences with gender. For example, we must become familiar with the many varied forms that masculinity can take and the extent to which, at various times and under various circumstances, gender is more or less salient in men's lives.[21]

Third, it is imperative that we begin to include previously excluded worldviews in our analyses. The relationships between hegemonic masculinity and other, subordinate masculinities can reveal much about the power relations embedded in the gender order—power relations that also contribute to the subordination of women. Gender as a social structure can be better theorized and visualized if we investigate the multiple ways that diverse lives are affected by it. While we may not always be able to conceptualize the minutiae of the entire structure at once, we need to keep the idea of the entire structure in mind at all times.[22] As components of a structure or system, femininities and masculinities are relational so that changes arising from, or happening to, any segment of the structure will likely affect other segments.

Certain of these sites of change have important implications in terms of providing common ground for feminist women and men to collaborate in disassembling patriarchy.[23] Until we learn to articulate them better, men's complaints regarding the gender system may sound very much like Betty Friedan's now famous "Problem That Has No Name." She coined this descriptive phrase to represent the vague feelings of unrest and incompleteness felt by the women in her research. These were women who, by all objective standards, were living the American middle-class dream yet were silently suffering under the yoke of imposed gender restrictions. Friedan writes:

> How can any woman see the whole truth within the bounds of her own life? How can she believe that voice inside herself, when it denies the conventional, accepted truths by which she has been living? And yet the women I have talked to, who are finally listening to that inner voice, seem in some incredible way to be groping through to a truth that has defied the experts.[24]

Finally, the places where we find men doing women's work may be sites where masculinity comes under great strain, presenting opportunities to add to our knowledge of non-hegemonic as well as hegemonic masculinities. Jim Allan, who has also studied men elementary teachers, suggests that the "fewness of men" in elementary teaching makes it a likely site for contradictions to emerge.[25] Estelle Disch agrees, writing in her introduction to her multicultural anthology:

> Unless we focus on the few alongside the many, we not only lose the voices of the few, but we also lose any meaningful understanding of the relationship between the few and the many, particularly in terms of power, privilege, disempowerment, and empowerment.[26]

It is also likely that, as David Morgan believes, biographies of non-hegemonic men may reveal possibilities for transforming the gender order that we would not discover in the biographies of the "usual central figures," who are likely to support standards of hegemony.[27] Many men experience life as being simultaneously marginalized and dominant.

Analytical projects resulting from such questions will be both unusual and challenging. Various feminist approaches assume that women experience a "symmetry" between their feelings of power-lessness and their objective lack of power;[28] however, a critique of masculinity that imposes this symmetry on men—that is, we have power; therefore, we feel powerful—is fraught with problems. So, too, would be a simplistic symmetry between the subjective, situational feelings of powerlessness of some men and a notion that they have no way to access sources of power. But having access to power is entirely different from normative, routine use of power. The difference lies in what must be given up, and this is revealed in the particulars of men's lives. For example, the men in my study would have to give up their connections to children to pursue more lucrative and socially powerful occupations. The men's own stories will reveal that such an exchange is unacceptable.

A feminist critique of masculinities that focuses on marginalized and subordinated masculinities could accomplish three things. First, we could "decenter" hegemonic masculinity, creating a view of masculinity from a different perspective. Second, we could develop additional theoretical frameworks that examine the ways that the politics of social class, race, ethnicity, and sexuality interact with those of gender. Third, we could formulate a sociology of masculinity that is grounded in the experiences of marginalized and subordinated men and would focus on the power relations in their lives. In this way, we are as likely to challenge the existing gender order as we are to conclude that individual men must change.[29]

We have to guard against assuming false commonalty among men. Scott Coltrane suggests that "standpoint" feminist theorizing can help us study men and masculinity by examining how specific activities structure consciousness. The emphasis here is on the societal forces that affect men's accomplishment of gender rather than on individual men's psychological needs to prove masculinity or feel manly. So Coltrane's question becomes, under what structural conditions are people likely to work at accomplishing their gender (to "do" gender)? I would add: and what gender will they accomplish?

Why would men want to study gender? Because it is important. It is a social structure at both the macro (institutional) and micro (interpersonal) levels. According to Coltrane, there are three ways to integrate men's standpoints into gender studies: (1) focus on men's emotions—don't accept outward expressions, for we may lack a vocabulary for describing our feelings; (2) study men in groups since we often have access when women don't; and (3) put men's experiences in a structural context. He suggests we could look at activities typically performed by women and the effects on men who do them.[30] As an example, Art, one of the first grade teachers in my study, shared the following anecdote with me. It is a scenario with which I am very familiar and one with which I wager any dad who has spent time as his children's primary parent can relate.

> Art: Some things really get to me, and I never know whether to speak up or just let them slide. I took my daughter [four years old] to the doctor for a follow-up exam. While we were waiting, I watched the nurse come out and call back several kids and their moms. When it was Katie's turn, the nurse told me to wait and she'd come get me "when we're ready." I don't get it. I was the only man in the waiting room and the only adult not accompanied by a child. I didn't dare complain, though.

This episode resonates with my own experiences at the doctor's. The only difference was that I did not remain silent and instead insisted that I accompany my child as all the other parents had done. It may seem like a small matter, but it is such particulars that must be the focus of our attention in order to ferret out all of the "rules" and assumptions that support the gender order.

The contradictions present in the lives of non-hegemonic men are likely to be most evident in the stories of men who can be defined as least representative of hegemonic masculinity. Gay men, unemployed men, men with disabilities, and men of color all fall into this category. So, too, do men who stay home and care for children or elderly relatives or who do women's work. These are situations where masculinity can come under strain. In pursuing life history studies, Robert Connell purposely selected men "for whom the construction or integration of masculinity was under pressure."[31]

Strain is found in the ambiguities and ambivalence surrounding men who do not display stereotypically masculine behaviors or desires. There is ample evidence that, starting at a young age, boys are more powerfully sanctioned for doing feminine things (acting sissy) than girls are for doing masculine things (being tomboy).[32] Little girls are often encouraged to participate in "boy" activities such as vigorous and/or contact sports, intense competition, and occupationally oriented play such as "firefighter." Later in life men who do not fit the mold of hegemonic masculinity are looked upon with suspicion or even considered dangerous.[33] Ironically, men who try to conduct their lives in non-sexist, atypical ways may find themselves under suspicion from both hegemonic men and many women. Being different exacts a great price for men and makes our lives very complicated and unsettling.[34] A man who is not quite "one of the boys," because of his social position, his sexual orientation, his taste in clothes, or his lack of leadership quality, aggression, or drive, may be looked upon with suspicion. It is this suspicion that makes the "rules of masculinity" visible.[35]

We may all simply be making the easier choice, responding to what "may not look like the exercise of power, but it is, in its most insidious form: the structuring of choices so as to make one choice 'obvious,'" such as choosing a baritone horn over a violin.[36] What happens when men make the more difficult choice to do "women's work?" This book is dedicated to that question.

A History of the Project

Several years ago, during the summer, I undertook what was at the time a fairly straightforward independent project to earn some units required for my master's degree. Since I was interested in the intersection of gendered lives and gendered workplaces, I wanted to speak with people who were working in an environment in which one sex predominates. Coincidentally, a group of elementary school teachers was on campus for a series of summer continuing education sessions. Using a rudimentary instrument that required open-ended responses, I asked as many of the teachers as I could to please tell me, in writing, what they liked most and least about teaching and to describe what, if anything, they would change about the occupation.

Generally, there was little difference between the answers provided by the thirty-three women teachers and those given by the fourteen men. "Making a difference in the lives of children," "watching children grow," "having summers (or some block of time) off," and "having time for family," with some variations, were mentioned on the majority of the surveys in response to what they liked most.

To the question of what they liked least, answers involving respect, pay, career ladder, control over curriculum design and content, and general isolation were sprinkled generously throughout the forms, again with no discernible association with gender. As I inspected the answers a little more closely, however, I found that some remarks did occur only on men teachers' forms. These concerned matters of "having all the discipline problems," "being the back-up custodian," and "needing a chaperone all the time." I had not anticipated such nuts-and-bolts responses and, since I am not an elementary school teacher, I wasn't sure what these rather terse statements actually meant. They left me confused and more than a little frustrated because I had no way to track down my anonymous informants and ask them to expand on their answers.

On the one hand, I eventually explained in my paper, I found no difference in the rewards, both intrinsic and extrinsic, that were perceived by men and women despite the widely held stereotypes about gender differences in job importance.[37] On the other hand, there is evidence from the short narratives that the men experienced differential treatment from either the formal or informal practices of the workplace. Christine Williams had found that men in traditionally female occupations experienced none of the kinds of discrimination and resistance that women in male occupations do. Instead, she claimed, men were more likely to experience negative self-image problems as they attempted to justify their position doing jobs traditionally done by women. In other words, the men were forced to negotiate an acceptable masculinity despite their immersion in a feminized activity. Williams' conclusions, from her study of women Marines and men nurses, are that (1) any discrimination the men experience is rooted outside the profession, (2) inside, men actually enjoy an advantage in terms of greater promotional opportunities and closer guidance from male superiors, (3) men experience less sexual harassment than women, and (4) men must "do gender" in ways that preserve and protect *their own* notions of masculine identity.[38]

My interpretation of the teachers' responses was that they were saying there were conditions and practices embedded within the work itself that differentially affected men and women. In other words, they were being treated differently, and this resulted in some significant obstacles in their teaching experiences. It was, however, impossible for me to follow up on this interpretation with the informants themselves.

The following year, while conducting an unrelated research project, I again visited elementary classrooms. I discussed some of my earlier findings, themes, and interpretations with the one man teacher (out of seven teachers) who accompanied me. Although he didn't confirm all of the issues I'd discovered, he quite candidly told me that there were things he had learned to "accept without question." He would only tell me that a few tasks were routinely assigned to men and that he had learned long ago that he could not get as close to the children as the women teachers could.

When I needed a topic for a seminar on work and occupations, I returned to the elementary school site and interviewed five men teachers. The purpose of the interviews was to determine the reason so many men elementary school teachers sought and attained administrative positions. This fact was in vogue at the time as part of the general "work and gender" area of the social sciences.[39] The commonly accepted explanation for men's advancement was the ability of men to take advantage of the patriarchal system of male privilege to move into more prestigious, powerful, and lucrative positions within a predominantly female field. For example, Williams spoke with men in various feminized occupations and, from her interpretations, coined the term "glass escalator" to help us envision the process by which hidden advantages facilitate men's successes in women's occupations. This explanation fit so well with theories of patriarchal pervasiveness that it received little critique in mainstream scholarship.[40]

I came away from the early interviews with mixed impressions. While it did seem as though a disproportionate number of men teachers reportedly became principals compared to women, the reasons were not as clear-cut as one might expect from reading the existing literature. I got a distinct impression of situations often pushing men out of teaching in addition to pulling them into more powerful and lucrative positions. They appeared to have entered teaching for one purpose, to teach, not to access a fast track to administration. In addition, of the five men I interviewed, three worked with women principals, one worked with a principal whom he described only as an "ex-high school coach," and only one described having any relationship at all with a man principal. This last man, Brad, portrayed the relationship between him and the principal as friendly, but formal.

> We're the only males on campus, so we do sort of tend to get together to talk. I don't think we talk about anything in particular, usually just school stuff, that last meeting, how a policy is working out. I don't even know why we do it. I guess because we don't want to ignore the only other male.

This "only male on campus" issue proved to be a fairly universal theme that has wide-ranging implications for the men's sense of integration and access to meaningful conversation concerning their experiences.

Probably the most powerful theme that emerged was the idea that the men had to teach differently than the women. While only one of the men taught at the primary level (K-3), they all described being constantly "on guard" around the children. They all stated that men are more suspect than women in their interactions with small children. Three of the men told me that others in their profession openly suggested that they should look at other positions, away from the small children. These alternative positions included administrative posts, specialty teaching, and upper grades.

By the time I had completed these five interviews my sociological imagination was piqued. The issue of low participation of adult men in the rearing and socialization of children is important to me, and I define as problematic any indication of a tendency to reduce men's contact with children. I'm particularly critical of any mechanisms that might reinforce a "men don't belong with children" stereotype. From each of my earlier projects, I had moved on, thinking I'd left the issue behind. I found, however, that I was clearly being pulled in deeper by the in-depth interviews. I still had unanswered questions, and there were other reasons. Something else was tugging at me, something I couldn't quite define, but that definitely created a sense of dissonance. For example, I got the impression that these men felt caught between serving the needs of the children entrusted to them and meeting societal expectations of masculinity. There was also a strong aura of anxiety over being watched closely in their interactions with the children, along with a certain resentment despite "understanding" the reasons for it. In addition, other people in their lives seemed more intent on getting the teachers promoted than the teachers themselves did.

Eventually, it became clear to me that the topic for my doctoral dissertation had presented itself. I outlined my research questions as follows:

- Are there structures, values or practices in elementary schools that act to keep men out?
- Is elementary school teaching so gendered that men really don't fit well?
- Once men enter the occupation, what happens to them?
- How do they interpret and react to the things that happen?
- How do they perceive their own identities?
- Finally, what was it that was not being said, and why wasn't it?

Armed with directories of local school districts, I sent out letters to every man primary grade teacher I could identify within driving distance. Ultimately I interviewed thirty-five men, all from different schools within five different school districts. Four of the men agreed to be re-interviewed. Additionally, I facilitated two three-person focus groups after the men had the opportunity to read a preliminary draft of the emerging themes. In addition to providing me an opportunity to listen to the men discuss their lives in their own language, the groups served as a form of member validation.[41]

My experience with the initial five interviews had led me to conclude that my research would be particularly interesting at the earliest grades since that is where men are the scarcest and where the children need a considerable amount of nurturing and care, stereotypically unmasculine characteristics. These men's work lives proved to be an area in which the institutionalization of masculinity was coming under strain.[42]

The Teachers and Me

One of my goals at the outset of this project was to be critical of the research process itself. This includes two important factors: the methods I used and the relationship between the participants and me. These phenomena are not mutually exclusive, but interdependent. In this section, I present a description and analysis of the interactions between the teachers and myself. An explanation and critique of the methods themselves are presented in Chapter Seven.

Several variables combine to influence the outcome of a research venture. The most widely examined include, but are not limited to, the race, class, sex, and sexual orientation of all involved. In addition, the way the participants perceive the purpose of the research and the influence of the methods used on the interaction between participants must also be considered. I will take these issues up in order.[43]

My own status as a white, heterosexual, middle-class, male agent of the university cannot be ignored. Some of the participants are not white, some are gay, and the pay of teachers does not support more than a working-class lifestyle (teachers' self-definition). My attachment to the university system presented other important issues. First, there is a perceived prestige difference between elementary and university teaching. Second, the men see the university as a source of some of their problems, as I will discuss later.

Peggy McIntosh presents a vivid account of coming to realize that her "whiteness" provided her with many privileges of which she was unaware until exposure to women's studies gave her a way and reason to critique the social order. At first, she saw only the mechanisms that oppressed her as a woman. Eventually, she saw that similar forces privileged her for being white. It is this set of privileges that often goes unnoticed and, therefore, unexamined in day-to-day affairs. Her model, consisting of forty-six privileges that accumulate on the side of whites in our society, can be applied to any of the groups represented in Audre Lorde's "mythical norm." Lorde writes that being white, heterosexual, middle class, Protestant, and male is the standard against which each of us is measured, even when we are unaware of the assessment process. In fact, we are likely to unconsciously measure ourselves against these criteria.[44]

Although I will not reproduce McIntosh's entire list, I believe some reflection on a few of her entries is instructive.

- I can, if I wish, arrange to be in the company of people of my race most of the time.
- I can avoid spending time with people whom I was trained to mistrust and who have learned to mistrust my kind or me.
- I can be fairly sure of having my voice heard in a group in which I am the only member of my race.
- I am never asked to speak for all the people of my racial group.
- I can go home from most meetings of organizations I belong to feeling somewhat tied in, rather than isolated, out of place, outnumbered, un-

heard, held at a distance, or feared.
- I can take a job with an affirmative action employer without having my co-workers on the job suspect that I got it because of my race.
- I can think over many options—social, political, imaginative, or professional—without asking whether a person of my race would be accepted or allowed to do what I want to do.

I will refer to this list in later chapters as I present the important themes that emerged from the teachers' stories. For now, I simply want to call attention to what I feel is a common thread running through all the items on McIntosh's list. These are essentially unearned and generally unrecognized privileges.[45] Each one, taken alone, may seem insignificant, like the individual wires of Marilyn Frye's bird cage metaphor. Examining one wire in the cage's construction may lead us to believe that it can be circumnavigated or even broken through. When faced with the cumulative impact of all the wires, we encounter the reality of social constraints and the power of the "normative" nature of hegemony.[46] Frye makes use of the "door ceremony" (men opening doors for women) to demonstrate how seemingly insignificant practices are important to analyze because of their cumulative effect and their roots in gendered assumptions. We could just as easily include the "waiting room ceremony" I recounted earlier.

Members of the most superordinate group will tend to see themselves as "neutral" actors in the midst of others whose attributes deserve some critical attention.[47] The group holding power assumes its perspective is one that is free of any influence *via* race, class, gender, sexuality, religion, and so forth. Members assume they are apprehending the world and its workings through untainted eyes and unbiased analysis. I need to examine the relationship between the teachers and me through the "matrix" of their and my various statuses. This meant that I had to be extremely aware of my own position and of the teachers' perceptions of it. Self-examination became a continual process in my analysis of my findings.

First, I had to examine my reason for doing this research, and had I not thought of doing this myself, I would quickly have been reminded to do so by the teachers who, being no strangers to scholarship and empirical research, simply asked me why I was pursuing such a project. Sometimes they wanted me to explain my hypotheses to them. Norman asked me, "So tell me, what is it you're trying to prove from all this? What's your hypothesis?" More often, the men just wanted to know what interested me about their situation, other than their obvious status as a numerical minority. The idea that their gender could be examined as a powerful organizing force in their lives, as it is in women's lives, was not something they had often considered. Chuck, a first-grade teacher, shows the taken-for-granted nature of having so few men in teaching.

> This seems like an odd topic for a dissertation. I mean, what are you looking for, besides the fact that there aren't many men? I thought it was common knowledge that men don't usually teach little kids. Why are you making a study out of it?

It is important at the outset to describe my own considerations of this question "why?" because of the potential impact of the answer on the relationship between me and the teachers and, more important, between me and my findings and conclusions. Put simply, I was involved in this research project to complete a dissertation that would enable me to earn my Ph.D. and to obtain a position in higher education. But that explanation too closely follows top-down deductive reasoning, as though I had first chosen to teach gender courses at the university level and then set out to fulfill all the requirements, including writing a gender-oriented piece of original research. It also ignores the wider context of my own personal and professional aspirations.

I have realized that certain phenomena interest and excite me. For example, I love to teach. In addition, the sociological perspective resonates well with my own worldview—developed long before taking any courses. The social construction of gender, specifically masculinities, seems to act as a dynamic pivotal point for my critical thinking about the social world. So to say I was doing this research "for the Ph.D." was simultaneously true and false. It is true in what it does say while its falsity lies in what it does not say. As I look over my notes, transcripts, and other material collected in this activity, I recognize a host of connections into my personal and emerging professional life, and these must be taken into account. This project is not floating free, disconnected from who I am.

In the interest of collaborative, egalitarian research, I chose to disclose as much of this to the teachers as possible.[48] Most of the time, this aided in creating a climate of open dialogue between equals. Occasionally, however, the men reverted to framing our interaction in terms of researcher/subject. I found this to be true whenever they found themselves struggling to describe what was for them an ambiguous concept. Mitigating against this response became another of my tasks. It is possible that, as men, we have become accustomed to interacting through our statuses, rather than as complete persons, and doing so becomes a fall-back position in times of stress, such as when we are posed a question to which an answer is not readily available yet we sense it should be. Perceiving that one is expected to have an answer to every question is perhaps another component of masculinity that crept undetected into the interviews.

Most of the time, something very interesting happened whenever I met with a teacher: two men disclosed experiences and feelings to each other. It required very little time to "warm up" to each other. Normally, a man will tell another that he is frightened or feels inadequate only in a few occasions so for this to happen between strangers is remarkable. I attribute this interaction to the men themselves, rather than to any interviewing techniques I used. I do, however, take credit for having consciously worked on letting my guard down over the years. I allowed the men free rein to express their feelings in whatever way was most comfortable for them and did my best to consistently demonstrate to them that I valued their expressions.[49]

As the research continued, I realized I was witnessing a group of men who did not live the lives of hegemonic, patriarchal males.

But why didn't they? They certainly weren't active gender revolutionaries. How was I to describe their situations? I was challenged to try to define these with existing vocabulary. These sessions were incredibly rewarding on both a professional and personal level. As a teacher I could see that they wanted to do for their students what I wanted to do for mine—get them excited about learning and develop a sense of pride. They were also unambiguous about loving children. As a father, I could relate to their expressions of love even if their language was not the same that women would use.[50] George, a second-grade teacher, said it best:

> Just being around these wonderful kids is a reward.
> They give back so much more than I give, I think.
> My kids are the same. I can't wait to get to them,
> to just be with them. Guys who don't have this are
> missing out. They're incomplete, I think.

The men acknowledged the magnitude of the problem of responding to the wide range of social and educational needs among the children in their classrooms. Many of the kids in their classrooms need "whole student" support, and this is very important to the men. In an environment in which the adults are expected, formally or not, to provide emotional support as a primary component of their job, it is possible that this may require a stress-filled dance along a very fine line for men.

Their own children provide experiences that help them teach better, and their students help them understand their own children better. Mostly, having children of their own created a congruence to their lives in which they could be the same kind of person at work and at home. Discussions about children were interwoven throughout their narratives. By discussing children, they have a path open to them that avoids stereotypical masculine topics and ways of speech.

I began listening carefully to how the topic of children was brought into their talk. In addition to references to their own children, they often told me about key events in their lives when they first had close encounters with children. Reading the existing literature had prepared me for this issue. The problem is, it had probably over-prepared me because I heard what I had expected to hear. Many of the men told me that they had little interaction with children for most of their lives until some event happened that put them in close contact with them. Typically, many told me that they "discovered that kids aren't so bad." I had anticipated this. As I listened very closely, however, I also heard them say that they had discovered that children might, after all, be safe in their care. I think this, more than any other discovery, convinced me that I was on the trail of new stories to add to those already available to us.

My Plan for the Book

This study examines what men elementary school teachers, particularly those in the primary grades, say they actually experience. I wanted to probe not only for information about experiences, but also for the men's feelings about those experiences and for what those experiences mean to them. I wanted to look at how the men construct their own masculinities on a daily basis, how they perceive their dramatic underrepresentation in the occupation, and what meanings this arrangement has for them.

In writing up the research, I wanted to use the findings as a frame for teaching about gender as well as teaching about men teachers specifically. For this reason, I have included more definitions and explanations than would typically be included in a book written for one's academic peers.

Chapter Two, "Crossing Over." I introduce some of the men who participated in this project. Their own descriptions of themselves, their backgrounds, their aspirations, and their feelings about teaching are mixed with social science descriptions of gendered occupations and gendered lives and the difficulties of doing gender when one is a drastic minority.

Chapter Three, "Under Scrutiny." The scrutiny under which the men must operate is the first theme presented because all other themes must be read through this in order to understand how they combine to structure the men's lives into work experiences different from those of women. The implications of policies that have disparate effects on women and men are discussed. Men's activities and the same activities performed by women are evaluated differently. "Women's laps are places of love. Men's are places of danger," says Keith, a first-grade teacher. Homophobia is presented as a mechanism of social control. In the face of intense scrutiny, the men develop compensatory activities that allow them to "be there" for the children without creating further suspicion.

Chapter Four, "Elementary School: A Gendered World." The men describe a workplace that is gendered both demographically and in terms of the division of labor. Important events with children mark turning points in their lives. In describing their career trajectories, the men also share their ideas about increasing the number of men in teaching. Their suggestions take us far from simplistic notions of increasing the pay and into the realm of media images and teacher recruitment and training.

Chapter Five, "Male Role Models." The issue of providing male role models, particularly for sons of single mothers, is ubiquitous in the literature of men and teaching. The men tell a different story from the usual picture, however, in that from their perspective several different, often conflicting, "models" are thrust upon them. Navigating among these models is complicated by the ever-present scrutiny.

Chapter Six, "The Culture of Primary Teaching." The men describe a culture in which they do not "fit" well. The general isolation experienced by classroom teachers is exacerbated for the men because of the scarcity of other men with whom to have dialogue and the lack of a vocabulary with which to describe their unique perspective. The scrutiny under which they must operate, the gendered division of labor, the ambiguity of providing male role models, and the strained relations with some of their women peers have a cumulative effect on the men. There are important implications associated with this research project. Fresh insights into the lives of men who lead gender-atypical lives were gained and new puzzles were generated that invite further research into this area, a fruitful source of information regarding the social construction of masculinities. I make the case that these men are part of a group that provides us with a unique standpoint—unique because of its apparently voluntary nature—from which to critique and eventually subvert the gender order.

Chapter 7, "The Research—A Personal and Professional Odyssey." This section is provided to give a detailed account of my methods and methodology. I've placed it at the end, rather than the beginning, since this type of material is primarily of interest to other sociologists and researchers. I left enough information about the research process within the main text for others to appreciate the major aspects of the project.

~ 2 ~

Crossing Over

Paul: Tell me about getting into teaching.

Jake: Oh my, where do you want me to start?

Paul: Anywhere you'd like.

Getting into Teaching

Thus began each of the forty-eight interviews (including the interviews with men enrolled in teacher education) that form the basis of this study. The ways that the men chose to structure their histories were as informative as the actual content of their narratives. "Getting into teaching" involved spending time pursuing unsatisfactory options, coming to new understandings about relations with children, and reaching back in time as well as out into the larger social world for reasons that their final choice should make sense. Before presenting each of these in order and comparing the men's stories with some available research on gender and organizations, I want to emphasize that these are honest stories, from the hearts of caring men. As I pointed out in the previous chapter, I felt an immediate connection with most of these men through the common experience of parenthood. This was true even when the teacher had no children of his own, but it was particularly the case with other dads. As I sat with Jake, from whose narrative I extracted the opening quote, his four-year-old daughter was as much a part of the interaction as he was. She was in and out of his lap, on and off the table, bringing us samples of her artwork and generally checking in every so often. Jake was ever-vigilant regarding her whereabouts and her activities. At one point in our talk we both stopped what we were doing and became silent for a moment. It was an automatic response on both our parts to the sense that his daughter was no longer in sight and there were no sounds to indicate her current activity. After he satisfied himself that she had not wandered off, we shared a warm moment and a nice laugh over our common experience with "parental radar"—that sense one develops, when caring for children, that there has occurred an unexplained interruption in the steady stream of sounds that should be present. This is not an inborn trait but a cultivated talent.

My opening query in each and every interview, "Tell me about getting into teaching," elicited the same basic response in almost every instance. First, each man alluded to the idea that the story would be a long and/or complex one. Second, like Jake, they all told me that they had not entered college, out of high school, with an eye toward someday teaching. They mostly described a work trajectory initially aimed at more stereotypically "masculine" occupations, which is not difficult to do since most jobs are "gendered" and the majority of jobs that provide the opportunity for high pay and status, which is where we are typically directed, are those occupied by men.

The quotes I've included aren't just answers to questions, but each participant's half of a conversation between men, men who are both teachers (and sometimes both dads) and therefore share a common set of experiences. Continuing with Jake's response:

> Originally I wanted to be an architect. I went to
> school, went to junior college. I just knew I wasn't
> going to be able to keep up so I changed my major
> to business and went to State U. and got a degree

in management at State U. and graduated just in time for a recession in the early '80s and didn't really find a job immediately, and I started doing some retail management. I managed a record store, managed a health food store, and kind of bummed around and realized, gee, this is really dead end, I'm not really going anywhere with this, and decided I wanted something else, so my mother had a friend who was a teacher, who said, "Well, come and observe teaching."

Jake's initial major, architecture, his second major, business management, and his early career positions are all examples of "men's work." The other men were similar in their descriptions. Dave was a rock and roll musician; John, a contractor; Adam, an engineer; Mike worked in manufacturing; and Dennis sold building materials. The men's initial college majors included architecture, engineering, business, math, computer science, physical education, biology, and chemistry. Men tend to be overrepresented in most of these disciplines.

John: I was a math major and just knew I'd be working in computers or science. Now it helps me show kindergartners how to put the right number of apples in the basket ... [chuckles] much more rewarding than debugging a program.

*****

Adam: After getting through most of the engineering program, it just hit me that I wasn't doing what I wanted ... what felt good. I was doing what I thought I should be doing. What my parents wanted ... what was "right."

Most workers in the United States are employed in occupations that are composed predominately of either women or men.[1] The local demographics of an occupation, organization, or job site tell only part of the story. Scholars such as Harriet Bradley, Rosabeth Moss Kanter, Barbara Reskin and Irene Padavic, and Christine Williams have clearly demonstrated that the "culture" of work can be gendered in the sense that normal practices are likely to be more conducive to one group's success than to others'.[2] By examining success stories, we make the genderedness of an organization visible, even if it had heretofore been hidden from the organization members themselves.[3] In explaining their change of major or occupation, the men used several versions of the idea that they simply did not fit in the original occupational milieus. Both Jerry, a twenty-six-year-old education student, and Dennis, a thirty-five-year-old ex-building supply sales representative, provide examples.

> Jerry: I was doing pretty good, with the course work [in architecture], the subject matter, you know? That wasn't the real problem.... I just couldn't get into the ... the mindset, for lack of a better term. It seemed like the other guys could translate what we were studying into their future ... could see themselves putting the stuff to work, into action. I just couldn't. No mental pictures came to me. I just didn't see this big successful architect in control of the design world. I was told that if I thought small I would fail.

*****

> Dennis: It seemed like I was the only one who couldn't get into it [selling] big time. I mean, it was just a job, not a reflection of who I was. I sold as much as they did, but I never took on the right persona, or whatever, never bought into that "go get 'em" thing.

Consistently, the men expressed the idea that they did not feel as though their original occupations matched their sense of who they are. They used descriptive phrases such as "uncomfortable," "stressful," "square peg in a round hole," and "odd man out" when trying to communicate their frustrations as they attempted to operate in a "masculine" work environment. Other researchers have also reported that the majority of men in their studies did not come to the profession along the same trajectory as women. However, most of the other investigators have concluded that men come to teaching as a kind of fall-back position after being unsuccessful elsewhere[4] or after discovering that children are not so bad after all.[5] Many men come to teaching because they conclude that there is a congruence between the needs of the profession and their own needs for self actualization. In addition, it is likely that these men actually discover that they do not represent the danger to children that we all have been raised to accept.

Because the phenomenon of gendered organizations has been recognized as an important locus of analysis for feminist research, considerable literature is available. Understandably the focus has been on the problems faced by women trying to enter predominately male jobs. To increase the opportunities for women and break down the barriers that exist between women and positions of power, privilege, and prestige, many scholars have called for an assessment of the manner by which we reconstitute the gender order on a regular basis. Of particular interest is the way we continue to reproduce the gender order through the sexual division of labor, especially the way we reproduce the hierarchy of gendered jobs and occupations.[6]

Rosabeth Moss Kanter examined the structural determinants within organizations that act either to empower or constrain people. By focusing on the experiences of women, she has discovered that the same determinants of women's failures have also been impeding some men as well, but because these forces were constructed around a worker base that was composed primarily of men the newcomers receive the full brunt of the restrictive and oppressive system. Most of the women at INDSCO, the pseudonym given to the corporation Kanter studied, were clustered into non-exempt positions, principally secretarial. The secretaries were, in Kanter's view, the very model of the oppressed worker.[7] The managers, on the other hand, more closely resembled hegemonic masculinity. Kanter cites Wilbert Moore's concept of "homosocial reproduction" in her evaluation of the dynamics of the managerial levels. Since management frequently operates within a framework of uncertainty, requiring a high degree of discretion, trust among management members is critical. The quickest way to trust is through homogeneity of experiences, values, and goals. New members who are perceived as being similar to the incumbents are deemed acceptable at the outset, while anyone who appears to be different must endure constant appraisal for signs of trustworthiness. In this way, characteristics that define one as different become salient.[8]

New minorities often adopt the roles identified by the majority in order to fit in. The majority define their own roles even more sharply because of the presence of the minority. Although Kanter's model sees "token status" as a more salient factor in organizational life than gender, her data clearly indicate that it is women who are the tokens at INDSCO. The organizational theory that emerges from Kanter's research has three major components, the ideas that (1) gender is embedded in organizational practices and policies; (2) positions held by women (minorities) lack power, advancement, and potential, so women lack power and can seem to lack the desire to advance; and (3) if women are employed in a "male" position, such as management, they will be treated as tokens, or representatives of their group, and may well come to self-identify with the token status. This identification process can create the appearance that marginalized workers actually enjoy functioning under a seemingly lower set of expectations.

Organizational structure is not gender-neutral. Normally, says Joan Acker, the structure assumes a male worker. One of the assumptions about men workers is that they will have no family responsibilities that could compete with work obligations. This assumption demonstrates the connection between the intra-organizational divisions of labor and the larger societal ones, or what Robert

Connell would describe as the connection between the "gender regime" of an organization and the "gender order" of a society.[9]

Gender is embedded in the normal practices of the organization. Some of the ways organizations are gendered—and thus gender the workers—include the routine practice of assigning certain tasks to either women or men, expressing an ideology (explicitly or tacitly) that supports the gendered division of labor, and perpetuating interactions between women and men that maintain power inequality. For example, Robin Leidner found that gender-segregated service jobs reinforce the perception of gender differences as natural. That is, gendered behavior is presented as inherent to the individuals themselves. Therefore, the argument continues, people are in jobs suited to their attributes. "All workers look for ways to reconcile the work they do with an identity they can accept."[10] It is remarkable how well we learn to construct gender in a way that it appears natural.

Gender segregation reinforces this appearance. If all the workers are one sex, or all the workers doing a particular set of tasks are of the same sex, it seems as though they must possess the special qualities required by the job. These findings are in agreement with what James Spradley and Brenda Mann found when studying cocktail waitresses and with Arlie Hochschild's findings when she interviewed and observed couples to gain an insight into the division of labor in the household. In each of these studies, the tasks within the social scene under investigation were divided by gender, the division was supported by ideologies accepted by the actors, the actors themselves supported a gender identity that fit the social scene in which they were functioning, and the overall sex/gender system itself remained unchallenged.[11]

I find it fascinating and instructive that the men in my study do not see themselves in stereotypically "masculine" ways. Their self-definitions, revealed through various segments of their narratives, more closely resemble what we define as "feminine."

> Pat: I'm just not comfortable with this whole competition thing. I mean, I've never liked it.

*****

Manuel: Being around kids brings out the best in me, I think. They need someone that's non-threatening, nurturing. I don't have to put on airs to being strong and aggressive.

*****

Don: I'm pretty artistic. Before, in my old job, I had to kinda keep it to myself, but with the kids, it's a real plus.

These are hardly the kinds of characteristics we typically associate with men. I can't help but wonder if they would so freely describe themselves this way had they chosen one of their original careers and I had been interviewing them as part of my inquiry into the lives of, say, engineers.

In the words of Manuel and Don, we see another factor that likely facilitated the ease with which the men communicated feelings, doubts, and other personal information—the way that the topic of children was woven into our talks. Talk becomes rich with intimate particulars of the here and now. It is nearly impossible to adequately describe children with a vocabulary consistent with "man talk."

Fred: It's just about impossible to spend time around these lovable little bundles, these little sweet faces, and not have a sense that all's right. I walk in in the morning and for the rest of the day I'm on the verge of either laughing or crying. They're so warm and wonderful.

Institutions can create and maintain differences between men and women, and these differences can result in unearned privilege being granted to one group over others. Employers often use sex stereotypes in designing jobs, and the resultant division of tasks reinforces the stereotypical notions regarding which jobs are supposedly naturally more suitable for women or for men. Reciprocally, men and women are thus seen as suited to different sets of particular tasks[12] and, as workers, will exert energy to ensure that the selves they present are consistent with the expectations of others, particularly those in power.[13]

Identities are negotiated until they make sense to everyone involved in the interaction.[14] Our genders are also constructed this way, by assigning meanings to gender differences and then relating to each other on the basis of those meanings. As Judith Lorber explains, "A taboo against the sameness of men and women divides the sexes into two mutually exclusive categories and thereby creates gender."[15]

Lorber tells us we start with two categories and then look for similarities within and differences between them. What we "see" is predicated on what we believe we *should* see. It would be better to assume that biological differences don't mean anything until we apply meaning through social practices. We should, perhaps, try to discover categories from similarities and differences in individual people's behaviors or responses, rather than start with the premise that mutually exclusive categories exist.[16] Organizational members may be influenced by the organizational culture to give signals to those who are perceived as different that the identity they are presenting is unacceptable. When marginalized group members feel threatened, they may actually withdraw and confirm negative stereotypes, suppressing their true feelings in order to provide a more acceptable presentation to the majority.[17] It's clear from the men teachers' stories that they regularly confirm several undesirable stereotypes in order to avoid suspicion.

Judith Gerson and Kathy Peiss, in conceptualizing the gender negotiations that transpire to create and maintain a division of labor by gender, tell us that we should look at the "boundaries" (specific gender rules) that are created in each social scene. They say that both women and men participate in negotiating these boundaries, and the question they ask is whether the resultant rules are more or less similar to traditional gender relations.[18] A good example of this would be Arlie Hochschild's study of married couples. By examining gaps between the participants' descriptions of the division of household labor and the reality revealed through observation, Hochschild was able to construct three family "types" having different sets of gender relations. Some couples were very traditional, some in transition to more equally involved roles, and a few were egalitarian.

Small changes in gender rules, while perhaps not significant in terms of producing changes in the larger gender system or in the societal division of labor, certainly have significant meaning for the individual(s) involved. The production of new rules is accompanied by the emergence of new forms of consciousness. Of course, not all boundary changes serve to challenge the existing order. In some circumstances, the dominant group may reinforce the boundaries through emphasis on differences, both real and imagined, and reinforce the idea that the occupation is more appropriate for one sex than the other. While both men and women in nontraditional jobs may experience opposition, harassment, and teasing, men may begin to exaggerate stereotypically masculine kinds of ideologies such as pursuing upward mobility, which is consistent with stereotypical views of maleness. Gender differentiation persists, then, as a social process that exaggerates the differences between males and females and creates new ones where no natural ones exist.[19]

The ways that organizations are gendered, produce gender, and are linked to the general societal division of labor may explain why, for many feminists, the gendered division of labor is seen as the basis for the subordination of women. Heidi Hartmann, in exploring the relationship between patriarchal ideology and capitalism, suggests that there is an affinity between the stereotypical characteristics associated with masculinity and the needs of capitalism. It is through socialization, she contends, that men take up these characteristics and by doing so ensure their opportunity for success. Sandra Harding explains that the societal division of labor that puts children into the exclusive care of women not only supports, but creates, patriarchal ideas as children learn their gender identity.[20] Girls learn to parent and boys learn not to.

Taking the mothering-capitalism connection a bit further, Nancy Chodorow, using Freudian theories of child development, says that women, through mothering, reproduce workers for the capitalist system in addition to reproducing more mothers. In this way, there is a sex-based division of values as well as division of labor that must be addressed. Philip Slater stresses this division in his thesis that males are socialized to be productive workers in the capitalist system. Further, he suggests that men may have no identity whatsoever outside the world of work. He details the kinds of personality traits that are most functional in the capitalist work world and demonstrates the price men pay in terms of limited emotionality and expression, leading ultimately to what Slater labels "loneliness," the logical and devastating endpoint of the quest for individualism.[21]

> Orin: You know, I watched my dad work until he dropped dead, and one day it just hit me, "Hey! I'm following right behind him."

*****

> Allen: I looked around one day and realized I didn't have a single meaningful emotional connection to anyone.

Gender is accomplished by individual women and men either in concert with, or in opposition to, prevailing gender ideologies and structures. In other words, we do gender in organizations while the organizations continue to "gender" us.[22] I will turn now to the ways that we do gender when we are immersed in a social scene that does not support our accomplishment. Specifically, I want to examine the possibility that men who work in nontraditional occupations are faced with more structural and interpersonal obstacles to accomplishing gender than those engaged in gender-typical activities. In general, we should be looking at organizational rather than at individual factors because they impact the workers' behaviors. However, to "see" these organizational factors, we may have to view the organization from the perspective of the individuals.[23]

Men Teachers

Several researchers have looked at the phenomenon of men working in predominately female occupations.[24] I use the term "predominately female" rather than "female dominated" to reflect the reality of the inequality of power in the public sphere. In occupations such as nursing, social work, librarianship, child care, and elementary teaching the majority of workers are women, but the major policymakers are men.

Elementary school teaching is a gendered occupation. In the United States, eighty-eight percent of elementary school teachers and seventy percent of elementary school principals are women. In the primary grades (kindergarten through third), women comprise ninety-eight percent of the teachers.[25] The elementary school environment has been described as a site of children's transition from the family to the public sphere with an emphasis on nurturing as well as curriculum in the K-3 grades.[26] The proportion of men teaching these early grades has not changed significantly in forty years.

The subjective experiences of the men who teach at the primary level are a potentially rich source of information that could increase our understanding of contradictory "standpoints." The combined effect of these perspectives will be a more robust theoretical base from which to disassemble the sex/gender system that currently supports, and is supported by, the societal division of labor.

Christine Williams and Jim Allan are two researchers who have looked into the lives of men teachers and whose work provides a starting point for my research. Both researchers employ descriptive metaphors to communicate important aspects of their findings, and it is at the intersection of these pictures that my research takes shape. Williams interviewed seventy-six men (along with twenty-three women) employed as nurses, librarians, social workers, and elementary teachers and describes their experiences in terms of a "Glass Escalator," or set of hidden advantages for men doing women's work. Based on his interviews with fifteen men teachers, Allan uses the title "Anomaly as Exemplar" to express the idea that men in elementary teaching, the focus of his research, experience contradictions in their teaching and gender roles.[27]

There are themes shared by both Williams and Allan, and there are issues that are unique to each work. Both address the possibility that a preference exists for hiring men and that men are over-represented in promotions. Both express these phenomena in terms of advantages and tie these advantages, to a lesser or greater extent, to the assumption that men can form allegiances with male administrators. Men in both studies are reported to have identified some tasks that are designated, either formally or informally, as gender-specific. The men also reported being under more scrutiny and suspicion than their women peers. Finally, men in both studies said that they performed some of their teaching tasks differently than women teachers performed them.

Of the two researchers, Allan is more likely to utilize phenomena outside of the men themselves to explain men's low participation in women's work. He explicitly problematizes the contradictory position in which men find themselves trying to construct "a meaning and a masculinity that fits the social situations."[28] The social situations to which he refers are the proscriptions and prescriptions regarding masculinity that are held by people important in the lives of teachers—peers, administrators, and parents of students.

Williams, on the other hand, sees most of the bias against men in women's work coming from "outsiders," that is, persons outside the field itself. She cites the men's families and the public at large as examples of outsiders. In addition, several other themes emerge from her work. First, she tells us the men are aware of the apparent ease with which men can be promoted to higher positions within female occupations, and this is often the motivation for entering the field. Second, men supposedly enjoy a kind of peaceful coexistence with female coworkers as compared with women in predominately male occupations who experience discrimination and harassment. Finally, the major concern for men in women's work, according to Williams, is the psychological stress of operating outside the norms of masculinity. She contends that men often promote upward to "resolve internal conflicts involving their masculinity."[29]

These two projects raise several important research issues. First, it is remarkable that both accept the notion that there is a preference for hiring men, since there is no empirical evidence to support such a claim. The proportion of men in primary teaching has not increased in several decades. In fact, Allan himself states "the proportion of males has actually declined over the last twenty years."[30] Second, neither Williams nor Allan vigorously pursue the effects of promotions on the men's sense of identity as teachers. Third, despite data from both studies that show the men may, in fact, experience a form of harassment from their peers and institutionalized discrimination via formal and informal practices, these issues are not explored in depth.

Williams explicitly states that the promotions that men receive are, after all, a positive consequence of the gendered nature of the occupation. She may be uncritically accepting traditional, bureaucratic definitions of success, based on promotions and accumulation of power, rather than deferring to the teachers' definitions of the situation. As the men themselves will reveal, promotions are often a matter of escaping the pressure of scrutiny, rather than pursuing the dream of advancement.

Allan has built a substantial portion of his conclusions and interpretations on the idea that men teachers have close relationships with men principals. Statistics, however, indicate that less than thirty percent of elementary principals in the United States are men.[31]

Both Williams and Allan have uncovered the important concept that men who teach small children find themselves faced with the daunting task of "doing masculinity" under circumstances that outline a very narrow field of play. We need to know even more about how these men define, make sense of, and navigate these rough waters, and we need to ask them for richer descriptions of the constraints, sanctions, or opportunities that they perceive are present. In this way, we will have a better understanding of the choices they make.

Specifically, my objective in this research is to follow up on the issues raised by Williams and Allan concerning promotions, reactions of others in the workplace to "maleness," the gendered division of labor in the workplace, and men's perceptions of doing masculinity under a variety of circumstances. There are possibly conditions under which gender becomes very salient and times when it is less so.

I also wanted to discover more about what is not being said. For example, how have the men been received when, or if, they have questioned any of the constraints placed on them regarding physical contact with the children? If they have not questioned any of the issues they've described, why haven't they?

The proscriptions against "doing anything feminine"[32] or against being close to the children carry far more serious implications than simply causing others to question the men's masculinity—and thus resulting in them questioning their own manhood. Suspicions of homosexuality and the conflation of gayness with pedophilia are powerful sanctions that carry legal implications. Loss of one's job and threats of jail time can bring even the most rebellious gender outlaw into line. In the group interviews all the men acknowledged learning of men who lost their jobs or were made to feel so uncomfortable that they moved on. Several knew of at least one man in their respective districts who opted to leave teaching rather than go through a public hearing that would traumatize him and his family.

Both Williams and Allan point out that these concerns are present in the interviews they did with men teachers, but neither researcher sufficiently explores the effects of these issues on men's actions and decisions.

In addition, if, at the lowest grade levels, nurturing behavior on the part of the teachers is considered to be a necessary component of the educational experience, how do men feel about their accomplishments as teachers if they feel they are constrained from providing this component? They may feel they provide nurturing in ways different from their women peers. A large part of my research puzzle is to discover how the men negotiate their identity as teachers as well as their identity as men since these two identities are perceived as contradictory.

At what point might some men abandon all hope of proving that they are "real" teachers? The notion that men, once they conclude they cannot be real teachers, can move up in the profession should not be accepted at face value. I intend to problematize that process rather than conceptualize it in terms of positive changes in men's or children's lives. To accept promotions as positive is supportive of the ideology that men are, and should be, oriented toward narrow definitions of success and upward mobility.

> Jeff: I plan to be teaching little kids until I'm old and gray. And I will be, unless things get even more stifling. If I feel that they've driven me away from the kids entirely, then I might look into being a principal or something. Probably not. I'll probably just go do something else. I couldn't stand to be around the kids and not teach.

~ 3 ~

Under Scrutiny

Women's laps are places of love.
Men's are places of danger.
                    —Keith, a first-grade teacher

The theme that elicited the most emotional responses from the teachers was that of having to work with children under a cloud of suspicion. Almost every teacher spoke of his reluctance to be physically in contact with the children because the action might be misconstrued. Touching the children, the teachers told me, can be taken as a sign the men are pedophiles or are gay. Often these two are inextricably conflated in ways that can be only partially explained through this research.

Because of the scrutiny under which they must perform, many of the men have chosen to adopt what I call "compensatory activities" that allow them to partially make up for what they feel the children lose when the men distance themselves. These activities help to reproduce the image of men teaching differently and add to the general suspicion about those who do not adopt these behaviors.

The practice of suspecting men is so deeply embedded in the school culture that the men simply do not question it openly even though, as revealed in their stories, they have serious concerns. In the focus groups, this issue was discussed in detail, and it was then that I became aware of the language being used by the men. By comparing their individual stories with their group stories I discovered the powerful emotions they hide regarding this aspect of teaching.

Touching

According to the teachers, most school districts have adopted policies regarding contact with children. Whether these policies are related to issues of molestation, corporal punishment, or simply invasion of privacy, each district has in one way or another instructed personnel on how to negotiate the issue of being close enough to respond to students' needs while maintaining enough distance to protect teachers and the district from any legal claims. All of the teachers I interviewed contend that these policies are enforced differently for men and women. Although many of the teachers claim that they understand the greater concern over male personnel, they also state that this differential application results in significant modifications in their approach to teaching. These modifications very likely exacerbate the appearance of difference between the men and their women peers.

The men do not touch the children in the same way that their women peers do. They are reluctant to be seen having any physical contact whatsoever with the children. Most acknowledge that this is not a perfect situation for the children since it does not provide the kind of close attention and emotional support that the children really need. Even when the official policies do not appear to dictate this difference, the informal practices do.

> Bill: In the classroom situation it's difficult because I'm in a public place dealing with children who aren't mine, and another stereotype of males is that males are child abusers and sexual maniacs or frustrated sexually. So I am held to a tighter standard and watched more carefully how I interact with children physically, and possibly dialogue

also, verbally. So, I don't initiate any type of physical contact at all, and I don't put myself in a position to be alone with the child, either male or female, in the room.

*****

Paul: Do you physically touch them?

Chuck: Sometimes on the head. Or the shoulder. They come up and hug me, though I don't initiate hugs.

Paul: No? Why?

Chuck: Why? Um, given the current situation, I just don't think it's a good idea.

Paul: Good idea for anyone?

Chuck: Well, especially for a male teacher. It's a shame, too, because those kids really need it. Maybe they're not getting that attention at home.

Prohibitions against touching have consequences beyond affecting the men's teaching style and depriving the children of affection. They also reproduce the image of men as not being sources of love and nurturing, as Mike explains.

It's real difficult, especially at the elementary school level for male teachers who have ... who are ... I think most male teachers that teach the younger kids have a tendency to be nurturing males. And there's a lot of hugging and things with younger kids that get a lot of yells, but not a lot of hugs. Then they come here and ... well, they still don't get hugs if they're in a man's room. I think they learn men don't care.

Without a doubt, the act most seen as open to suspicion is having a child sit on a man's lap. While none of the men explained in detail what the specific significance of the lap was, most used it as a quintessential symbol of men stepping over the line in their interactions with the children.

> Bill: Females in this profession working with children are allowed by society, as a whole, teachers, parents, students, to be more physical with children. Female teachers at school can have a child sitting on their lap during class time, and very few people would give it a second thought. It's natural; it's common. No one would ever think that there was anything wrong going on. But, if someone walked into this room, and I had someone, a child, sitting on my lap, immediately some red flags would go up in most people's minds: "Is this right? Is this common?"

In Bill's comments we find two commonly expressed themes in addition to the danger that men represent. First, physical expressions of caring by women toward children are considered "natural," and second, the same act can be evaluated differently by an observer based on the sex of the actor.

> Dennis: It's not that I'm not nurturing, but as a male, you're crazy if you hold the kids and sit them on your lap. You're just opening yourself up for a lot of grief. So you have to be cognizant of the fact that you can't put a lot of the physical touch in the situation, and it's really understandable.

Dennis' remarks reveal he feels he is a nurturing person but must comply with proscriptions against men touching children. Like most of the men, he voiced agreement with the reasonableness of this proscription during our individual interview session.

> Jake: But there's things, like I would never put a child on my lap. I would feel uncomfortable with that. And for good reason, too. I mean it's not that I feel uncomfortable with it. I do it with my daughter all the time, but that's a whole different story. When you're a male and you're dealing with young children, you're always kind of under the microscope, because of the plethora of child molestations that occur, primarily by males. And so rather than being put in the position of being questioned about what I was doing, I'd rather just not even deal with it. The kids don't seem to suffer because of it. There are things I just don't do.

The men most often made direct reference to sexual molestation during these individual discussions of the difference between women's laps and men's laps. The child's close approximation to an adult man's genitals is clearly the issue.

> Keith: I really love these kids. You know, I just don't care any more. I mean, I know we're supposed to be kind of standoffish, but I can't be. These little folks need care and love and hugs. I even let them sit on my lap.

> Paul: Why "even"?

> Keith: Oh, that's the big no-no. *Women's laps are places of love. Men's are places of danger.*

Keith has probably come closest to defining the situation: "Women's laps are places of love. Men's are places of danger."
Throughout these interviews there was an ever-present idea that

men represent danger while women represent love and protection. The idea that "females equal safety and males equal danger" effectively denies the dangers of bad women teachers and the safety of loving men teachers. In addition, this adds one more duality or polar concept to the idea of separate spheres for men and women. There is more to be presented on this issue of sexual danger in the section on homosexuality and pedophilia.[1]

Alone With Children

Along with sitting on laps, being alone with children was listed as a serious misdeed. The difference, however, is that being alone carries a sense of impropriety somewhat more equal in its effect on men and women teachers. There was frequent reference to the sex of the child, however, with almost all the teachers who spoke on this theme using a female child as an example.

> Don: O.K., if I keep a female student after school, just for doing that I can get myself in trouble. I would have to have three or four—the more, the better. I want to have witnesses.

*****

> Mike: I mean so ... you know, you just have to be ... as a male teacher, you have to be more careful all the time. You have to make sure that you're not particularly in classrooms with just a girl without anybody else, you know, some other kids in the classroom.

Such comments are particularly intriguing considering that, as explained below, the men perceive an undercurrent of fear among school administrators, peers, parents, and the community at large that perhaps the men are homosexuals. But the men teachers also believe that they are seen as a potential danger to girls. As I will demonstrate under "events with children," the men have grown up under the yoke of assuming that they are always a possible danger, in many ways, to small children.

Gender also comes into play when arranging for other adults to assist in the care of the children. This resonates with my own experiences as a father of elementary school children.

> Bill: I try to have another adult in the room also, preferably an adult of the opposite sex. So I have a female aide, and I chose a female aide for that very reason, so that she can be another adult, another gender. So if anything ... if rumors start going around, she can verify what's really happening.

> Paul: When you say "rumors" going around ...

> Bill: If a child goes home and says I hugged Mr. Smith today, and the parent maybe misunderstands that and wants to know why is an adult male hugging my eight year old child, they come to me and they may not believe my side of the story, but I'll have an aide here to vouch for the kinds of behavior that happen in here.

*****

> Adam: The women can take off with their classes without another adult, and no one says anything. Let me do that, and I'd be up for discipline. I can't even have one of the kids' dads accompany me; it has to be a woman.

Many of the men, like Bill and Adam, told me that they feel as though they have to make special arrangements to accomplish what their women peers seemingly manage to do without much preparation. This idea of having to do more in order to fulfill job obligations arose in many forms throughout this project.

> Eduardo: It's no wonder that the kids feel better
> around the women. We have district guidelines
> about touching the children. Basically, if you don't
> have to, don't. The women fairly well ignore the
> rules, as they should; we all should. These kids
> need hugs and handholding at their age. The prob-
> lem is when the women do it, they're just doing
> what's natural. If I do it, I get hard looks.

Eduardo has exposed the contradiction between the formal rules and informal practices that can contribute to different experiences for men and women teachers. The notion that elementary teaching is an extension of women's "natural" talents and propensities frequently arises in the narratives of these men. When caretaking actions are labeled "natural," they are not rewarded. Barbara Reskin suggests that the social construction of primary teachers has been laden with the features that surround the construction of "mother" and "female." It is evident from these men's stories that this extension of the natu-ralness of teaching for women (mothers) contributes to the suspect nature of men in primary teaching.[2]

Christine Skelton, in addressing the issue of institutionalizing certain hiring practices to protect school children, says,

> The problem is how can it be ascertained during an
> interview the point at which a *male* candidate's
> espoused caring concern for the children's physical
> and emotional welfare crosses the boundary into
> abuse?[3]

So we are to believe that child abuse, for men, can be foreshad-owed by behaviors that are just a notch or two further along the car-ing continuum? If so, men are being told not to show too much care, specifically not to show as much care as a woman would (i.e., to avoid acting feminine). At the same time, Skelton warns, schools don't want a situation in which the women will have to be called on to do the men's nurturing work for them, thus adding to women teachers' workload. This frequently happens, not so much because men call on women to step in, but because the gendered division of labor in the teaching culture sets this expectation firmly in place. As will be shown in this research, several "male" duties are added to the men's teaching tasks as well.

Skelton goes on to describe a scenario in which a child is injured near the genitals. When this happens, a woman teacher is called on to chaperone the man's inspection. It is apparently unproblematic for women to inspect boys without a chaperone, because Skelton's point is that

> ... no discussion seems to have taken place on ini-
> tial teacher training programmes or by school gov-
> erning bodies as to how male teachers can interact
> effectively with young children in the area of phys-
> ical contact. This lack of open discussion can only
> contribute to the perpetuation of child sex abuse in
> primary and nursery schools.[4]

Once again, the image of the dangerous man implies the image of the nurturing, safe woman. Skelton calls for a specific naming of "child sex abuse" in the hopes that giving it a label that identifies it as separate from other abuses will "contribute to the initial screening of men" in light of the "interrelationship of masculinity, sexuality, and violence."[5]

By specifying that it is only men that need to be screened, Skelton leaves us with the notion that women never need screening. This is in agreement with the image of women teachers enacting the mother role to which I alluded when I described my memories of my own women teachers and my experiences with the elementary schools of my own children. There is little research to help us determine what message we give boys about their own bodies when women, but not men, can have unsupervised access to them. However, this arrangement clearly reinforces the notion that it is to women, and not men, to whom children must turn for intimate assistance. It also reinforces the boys' own image of their future limitations in this area. How are they to come to see themselves as care-takers when they do not see men caring for children?

Skelton draws on the work of Robert Connell, who contends that children learn more than just the academic curriculum in schools. Children learn gender roles and sexuality in addition to substantive learning. Children are also introduced to power inequalities, according to Skelton, creating the "greatest potential threat to children being able to cope in schools"; sexual abuse is defined as the epitome of this phenomenon. Skelton asserts that other forms of abuse, including physical and verbal, take place in front of witnesses. The men in my study discussed their concerns about this issue, and I've presented their views in the section devoted to the focus groups.[6]

Sources of Information

There are several official and unofficial sources of normative information for the men regarding physical contact with the children. Many, like Dennis, tell of an early mentor who clarified the expectations in order to prevent any problems arising in their young careers. A few of the men, such as Fred, now see themselves as mentors to new teachers and so pass the folk culture on.

> Dennis: Well, it's something that when I first came into education at the high school level, that I had a department head, a lady that was a former major in the army, and she was very frank and talked like a truck driver, made no bones about it. She said, "Look, you're a male. You're young, and you can't be in a room with a female student and not basically open yourself up for some situations, so whatever you must do, whenever you're talking, and especially when you have to have those communications one on one a lot of times and you're helping them out one on one, you need to keep the

door open. Always keep the door open; in fact, insist that it stays open."

*****

Fred: One morning I came walking by Tom (excellent teacher, he's now the assistant principal I talked about), and he was standing there with one of the girls, and, you know, he comes out of EST and New Wave and all this, and he's standing there giving her a pep talk, and I don't know if she was feeling down or something, but he was rubbing her back. It was in public and she had a shirt on, but he was standing there and, you know, massaging her back. I went up to him and said, "Tom, let's have a little talk."

Quite often it is the reaction of the parents, upon discovering that their child is to have a man teacher, that acts as a source, or reminder, of the special case of men in teaching. Although the parents don't often overtly express misgivings, the men can describe what they feel are clear signals.

Chuck [on why new parents were hanging around after the first day of school had begun]: I think I was young, and they probably just wanted to get a feel for me. You know, this is a person that their children will be spending six and a half hours a day with for 165 days a year. Natural concern.

Paul: What kinds of concerns do you think they might have?

Chuck: Just by what kind of a person I am. 'Cause this isn't, it's not a typically male field, so I'm sure they wondered.

> Allen: I can go back, I keep telling the story, to my
> very first year in the district. I had a first grade. The
> second day of school, there were six phone mes-
> sages in my mailbox for me, and they were from
> parents who wanted their child removed from my
> classroom because they were afraid of me.

Senior personnel appear to be a source of ongoing reminders
about the need to stay distanced from the children.

> Jake [explaining how he knew he was under
> scrutiny]: Because I've been warned by principals
> before. The principal at my school right now—we
> talked about that before—said, "Just watch your-
> self."

There are regular, institutionalized reminders, also. Although
the in-service sessions directed at reinforcing district policies appear
to be gender-neutral, it is clear that the men see their content as
being directed mostly toward them.

> Roger: No, no. I think as a professional, as a
> teacher, I can't have that anxiety simply because of
> my maleness. When young children want to ap-
> proach you and give you a hug, I think all you're
> doing is a disservice to them by saying, oh, I'm a
> man. You know, does that make that different? I
> don't think so. Um, of course, we're indoctrinated
> year after year after year, that, yeah, especially in
> the last ten years, you know, it's almost as though
> we have to go through a mandatory, every year
> thing. You know, "Be careful; be cautious." If you
> keep it in perspective and you understand.
>
> Paul: So all teachers attend?

> Roger: Yeah, but the emphasis is always on us
> men. They just say, "Look, it's a reality."

Roger is also one of the few men in this study who stated frankly that he felt it was necessary to defy and work around the rules and attend to the emotional needs of his students. There is great risk associated with doing this and in disclosing that he does. Sid tells us:

> I made the mistake of telling some of the teachers
> that I didn't give a damn about the rules and that I
> give kids what they need. The next day, Sally [his
> principal] called me in and told me that the rules
> are there to protect the district and the other teach-
> ers and I'd better comply if I wanted to continue
> teaching.

Homosexuality and Pedophilia

In addition to the image of "mother" cited earlier, Barbara Reskin tells us that there are also negative constructs such as "homosexual" and "pedophile" that are used to help structure the gendered nature of teaching. These are emotionally loaded terms and, while they are receiving extensive attention in both the popular and academic media, they can act as a kind of social control mechanism to keep the number of men teachers at a minimum.[7] The social construction of homophobia acts as a ritualized mechanism of social control, especially since it has been conveniently (and erroneously) conflated with pedophilia.[8]

> Dennis: But the thing that shocks me is the parents'
> approach. They immediately think that you're gay.
> That's one of the things that comes up and they ask
> questions in a round-about way. I just recently got
> married. For most of the years I hadn't gotten mar-
> ried and so they would not see a ring and they'd

look at my age and they'd go, "Oh, my gosh, this
guy's probably gay. I don't want a gay man teaching my children."

*****

John: Fortunately I've been successful as a kindergarten teacher, so I started to develop, in my past
school and this, a reputation of being good. And so
parents trust me. But they still in the back of their
mind go, "Why is this guy teaching young children? Why is a male...?" They really question that
quite a bit. Some of them will even be point blank
and say, "Why are you teaching here? Don't you
think you should be...? You're very strange to
teach."

Jim Allan, in constructing a continuum of masculinity, describes,
at one end, men who acknowledge their "feminine" aspects and in
fact celebrate them and know that there are others who will perceive
them as feminine. They also acknowledge that they are being paid
less because they are doing "women's work." The men in my study
are aware that if they celebrate their feminine aspects a little too
much and really show their caring and nurturing sides to children
then they become suspect. They know that, for men, nurturing children is judged dangerously close to molesting them. Young, single
men are particularly suspect, which may explain why young men
teachers are loath to call attention to throwing themselves into their
work. Women are praised, but a young man is suspect for not having
something more important to do, away from children. Allan says it's
ironic that the very aspects of masculinity that ought to be modeled—
responsibility and care for children—are the very things that are the
most suspect. Here we have the reproduction of absent fathers, a kind
of "back door" (indirect) reproduction of mothering. The title of Jim
Allan's paper, "Anomalies as Exemplars," reveals his sense of the
ambiguities associated with men in primary teaching.[9]
  Men and boys who violate dominant definitions of gender-
appropriate behavior are viewed negatively and treated with suspi-

cion.[10] Gregory Herek submits that they are stigmatized and that this stigmatization is the essence of heterosexism. One of Herek's goals is to describe how "symbolic statuses" rather than real experiences guide most people's perceptions of homosexuals. Many people have likely never really interacted with a homosexual nor a man primary teacher yet have pre-conceived notions about them.[11]

Despite the scarcity of molestation cases in the districts where I interviewed, the ever-present cautionary tales keep the men teachers both invisible and condemned, what Herek calls the "twin themes of denial and stigmatization."[12]

Judith Butler proposes that the illusion of separate, "core" genders is maintained through discourse for the purpose of social control, especially the regulation of sexuality within the obligatory frame of heterosexuality. Butler sees no reason to divide bodies into male and female sexes except to suit the economic and political needs of heterosexism. Men, such as homosexuals, who do not follow the standard behaviors culturally defined as "masculine" are negatively sanctioned. Homosexuals become a negative symbol of masculinity. This is done to enforce masculine gender traits among men and to ensure they continue to follow the masculine mandates.[13] Cathexis, the structure that organizes individuals' social attachments and where the individual invests desires, is thus distributed in ways that shortchange men both in terms of relationships with other men and, as shown in this study, in interactions with children.[14]

Both Michel Foucault and Gayle Rubin present the idea that sexuality must be understood socially and historically. Modern society has a hierarchical system of sexual values, and intergenerational relations, or adult-child sexuality, is perceived as the worst offense. Finding a woman with a child on her lap is likely to be framed in terms of being a normally occurring event (despite the official school position), whereas the same scenario, substituting a man for the woman, will add to the mountain of "proof" that shows men must be watched. "Save the children" and "homosexual menace" have become battle cries in contemporary U.S. society.[15]

It is through this "homophobia-as-social-control" model that the plight of the men teachers becomes clear. Each man teacher always has to negotiate between being a "real man" and being a "real teacher." Real men do nothing feminine. But the lower the grade level, the more feminine is thought the teaching. One of Jim Allan's informants from fifth grade was apprehensive about moving down to earlier grades. Allan uses this man as an example of the other end of the continuum of masculinity he has constructed. This second axis consists of men who define themselves in opposition to women by modeling a hyper masculinity and trying to avoid an association with homosexuality. Homophobia can be defined as men's fear of being seen as feminine.[16]

In the context of the above, however, it is justifiable for men to be fearful of any label that could, at the least, cost them their job and, in the worst case, cause them to be imprisoned. In the context of the teaching occupation, "avoiding anything feminine" may have less to do with proving manliness and more to do with escaping severe sanctions. L. Susan Williams and Wayne Villemez suggest that through a "social control" model of analysis, we can see that there are real obstacles to men's access to predominately female occupations.[17]

The men I interviewed are quite sensitive to the possibility of severe sanctions for any suspected offenses involving the children in their care. During the individual interviews, the topic of being under scrutiny was presented in matter-of-fact terms that demonstrated that the men accepted the rationale behind the disparate treatment. In the focus groups, however, as the men became more comfortable with each other's and my presence, strong feelings of resentment and injustice were revealed. For this reason, I am including a detailed description of the focus group interactions at this point. Once I became more aware of how central the issue of being under scrutiny is to these men, the other emerging themes became more important than they would otherwise have.

Focus Group Talk

I invited every teacher to participate in a focus group. Over half expressed a desire to meet with other teachers, but their busy lives made arranging such meetings difficult. However, two meetings with three teachers present at each did take place. Each teacher had the opportunity to read a draft of the emerging themes as I understood them before the meetings, and I invited them to be as critical as they wished of my interpretations of their experiences. I had anticipated that much of our meeting time would be devoted to this critique and could only hope that the agenda would eventually turn to the teachers discussing the content of my findings among themselves.

I was pleasantly surprised on both occasions when the discussion turned immediately to an exchange of thoughts and feelings about the substance of my findings. It was clear that the men thought my presentation to be fairly representative of the experiences of men teachers as these men saw them to be. This "member validation"[18] was wonderful and came at a time when I was feeling unsure of my ability to see the world through their eyes. I had been experiencing some doubt about my findings and interpretations and was fearful that I might be imposing my definition of the situation on the narratives contained in the transcripts.

The first focus group consisted of Eduardo, Javier, and Roger. Barry, Frank, and Nate attended the second. Two issues dominated the focus group discussions. The first to be brought up in both cases, and the one that occupied the majority of the time, was the issue of being under suspicion or scrutiny. The second was the issue of the behaviors and personalities of the women teachers in terms of interacting with children and with men teachers. The interactions with children will be discussed in this section, and relations with women peers is covered in Chapter Six. In addition, some discussion of the division of tasks and the ways to increase the number of men in teaching occurred. These final items, comprising a very small portion of the focus group interviews, were sprinkled throughout the discussion.

On both days, the discussion began with the men saying that they understand why they are more suspect than women. But as the sessions went on, their ambivalence regarding the issue became progressively more obvious. They certainly understand that child molestation and abuse occur and they firmly support guarding against either happening at school. However, they clearly are frustrated with what appears to be the lack of understanding on the part of peers, superiors, and the public of just how frustrating, demeaning, degrading, and constraining constant suspicion can be.

When the men first began their discussion of my findings, they immediately launched into a discussion of the issue of men being under scrutiny. It is interesting that mostly they talked about men in a kind of third-person format like distant observers.

> Javier: Men are more under the microscope than women. It's understandable. *They* are the ones abusing children.

*****

> Barry: Men are watched carefully around children. *They're* more likely to molest a kid than a woman is.

The dialogue became progressively more personal and "I" oriented as the men grew more comfortable with each other. As with my one-on-one interviews, I was struck with just how quickly this happened. A few of the men recognized each other from having seen each other at a work-related function, and some recognized each other's names, but only two men had actually had any interaction prior to the focus groups.

I noticed, in reviewing the transcripts of both focus groups, that at just about the same moment there was a shift to more personal accounts. Once the personal accounts began to flow, the description of the scrutiny phenomenon shifted from something that was "understandable given the seriousness of the problem" to an annoyance and hindrance to teaching. Finally the men's anger emerged. In the midst of the anger was the notion that being under suspicion changes their behavior. It makes them less likely to display the kinds of nurturing behaviors that might counteract the stereotypical image of men being non-nurturing or abusive. However, the men were also sensitive to the probability that if they did begin to show lots of nurturing behavior, the other mechanism of social control, homophobia, would be invoked and they would also find themselves under suspicion of molestation. This was presented as a "no win" situation. They described a very fine line along which they must navigate to escape the severe penalties awaiting any misstep.

As in the individual interviews, the issue of being labeled gay was significant. "Gayness," they thought, had two dimensions. First is the still prevalent notion that homosexuals will somehow pollute and pervert children's moral values and, perhaps, even influence some children into a gay lifestyle. Second, the idea that gay men are synonymous with molestation was thought by the men to be deeply ingrained in the general culture. The exchange between first-grade teacher Barry, second-grade teacher Frank, and Nate, a gay man who teaches third grade, is instructive.

> Barry: The first impression I get is that some of the parents assume I must be gay because I teach little kids.

> Nate: What do you think bothers them the most about that?

> Barry: My guess is they probably think I might molest their kids.

> Frank: I get the same feeling. The first thing they [parents] look at is my hand to see if I'm married.

> Nate: See, as a gay man, I feel folks are afraid I'm going to turn the kids gay. That's always with me. In some situations, I also feel like people are watching me very closely to make sure I don't molest the kids. If I happen to be close to a kid when someone comes in my class, I can just see their eyes measuring the distance between the child and me. If I pat a kid on the shoulder or something, their eyes just ZOOM in on my hand.

Frank: But is it all because of a fear of gay men? I
mean, aren't they just worried about men in general?

Barry: I think any man who says he wants to be
close to children is just suspect. Most of them don't
know exactly what to do with that, and they're just
looking for a label for their fears.

This is a graphic example of Gregory Herek's "Symbolic
Status." The difference in this situation is that these men are presenting the idea that the "folks" who are evaluating the men—
including parents and other school personnel—are using a construct
that is a hybrid of at least two symbolic statuses: homosexual male
and child molester.[19] By conflating the two, they have constructed a
Garfinkelesque "identikit" of the person they fear most to have
charge of their children. Many of the behaviors men teachers adopt
are intended to distance themselves from this symbolic status.[20]

Although the men want desperately to show that they are capable of the same kinds of close interaction as their women peers, they
are faced with serious systemic contradictions. They know they cannot be as close to the children as the women and purposely distance
themselves. In so doing, they participate in the reproduction of the
myth of stoic, distant men. This means they are participating in their
own marginalization. While stoicism and inexpressiveness are considered to be generalized attributes of men, these are clearly deviant
behaviors in the world of teaching young children. The men seem to
see the differential application of policy as a further insult. If women
"break the rules," they seemingly do so at no risk. This is explained
in terms of their just doing what comes naturally to them, and in this
particular social setting expressiveness is the norm.

Yet another dimension of the discrepancy, according to the men,
is that although they accept that molestation or sexual exploitation
of the children is serious, some of the men wonder why other kinds
of abuses are not also on the agenda. They point out that when an
incident such as corporal punishment or emotional damage from

name-calling occurs involving a woman teacher, it is handled quickly, efficiently, and quietly. Despite these events happening frequently, there is no perception of a "crime wave" being reported.

> Frank: I've been teaching second grade now since I started teaching. I guess I wanted to teach little kids all along. Actually I'm kind of offended by this constant reminder from other teachers and from the principal that, as a man, I have to be particularly careful how I behave with children. I know what has happened. I know, um, how do I say this. I understand, I guess, that there have been some horrible incidents and most of them have involved men, but you know there have been some pretty terrible incidents that involved women too. They're just not all over the headlines. Molestation is one issue but, you know, um, slapping the kids around, yelling, calling them names, demeaning them—that's pretty awful, too. And that happens more in the women's classrooms than in the men's classrooms, I've noticed. There isn't this big push on to make sure that women understand they're being, you know, watched more closely. I think that people just assume that because a child is in a class with a woman the child is safe. Hey, that's just not true. Look at the evidence.

*****

Nate: There have been no incidents of molestation or sexual abuse in [his district] since I've been working there. But not a week goes by that I don't hear of a parent complaining about a teacher's treatment of their kid. Either there's been name-calling or singling the kid out and making an example of him that makes the other kids ostracize him. Sometimes it has to do with pulling or pushing the

kid, even slapping a kid. But there's never a big
story leaked to the press or anything.

According to sources published on the topic, children are more
likely to be sexually abused at home than in school or day care.
Based on a sixteen-state study, Ching-Tung Wang and Deborah Daro
have reported that only two percent of confirmed cases occurred in
institutional settings. While sexual abuse affects nine out of every
thousand children, the American Association for the Protection of
Children reports that forty-seven out of every thousand U.S. children are victims of other forms of maltreatment.[21]

In a study of law enforcement reaction to women who sexually
abuse children, E.D. Nelson showed that police, prosecutors, and
judges all were inclined to view charges against women as suspect
because they didn't fit the profile of the "typical" offender. Women
didn't appear dangerous. When women and men committed the
same act on a child, the act was viewed as having almost opposite
meanings. In other words, women don't fit Harold Garfinkel's
"identikit" referred to above. It would be almost impossible for a
heterosexual (supposedly) female mother to fit into the same category as a homosexual male "non-mother."[22]

Several teachers throughout this study provided anecdotal evidence of hearing women teachers' voices across the schoolyard as
they yell at students. In the focus groups the men quickly noted that
the recipients of most of these teachers' yelling are boys, and this
became another distinct topic in the focus group interviews. Men
teachers frequently end up with "disciplinary problem" boys in their
classrooms. The thinking is that boys are disciplinary problems, and
men are assumed to be disciplinarians—and the men's classrooms
become known for a focus on discipline and order. Most of the men
in my study, however, indicate that some women are more likely to
dole out harsh discipline than the men teachers are.

Compensatory Activities

The men I interviewed see themselves as good teachers. They describe a wide range of pedagogical styles. Most told me that they want their students to become active, as opposed to passive, learners. They obviously delight in getting their students to engage in the learning process. Like "Raymond" in Renate Schulz's narrative history study of two men teachers, many of my teachers also consider themselves "legends" in their schools in one way or another.[23]

> Bill: Pretty much I'm considered the taskmaster. I get the students who really need to learn to bear down on their work.
>
> *****
>
> Roger: I think that they, uh, tend to focus and send students to you accordingly at times, which I welcome. I enjoy working with the, you know, with those boys who kind of drive the other teachers crazy. [Chuckles] I'm kind of the special placement room. I get a lot of special, special kids.

Much of this notoriety comes from their minority, or token, status. Deborah David and Robert Brannon, in their early work, *The Forty-Nine Percent Majority*, would describe this as the "Big Wheel" form of masculinity.[24] Or as Candace West and Don Zimmerman and others might explain, these men are "doing masculinity" in whatever ways the social context of a predominately female occupation will allow.[25] This could mean that men's attention to (obsession with?) social hierarchy leads them to want to be the best at performing some task or fulfilling some social role. According to this way of thinking, it is better to be seen as a front-runner in a minor activity than an "also-ran" in a more prestigious undertaking. It is also certainly possible that the men may be some of the most technically competent teachers in the primary grades. They seem to put considerable energy into becoming ever more competent.

Dennis: I attend as many conferences as I can. I think it's important that we stay up on current ideas in teaching. I think a lot of other men think so, too. I see more men at the conferences, ... also at the training sessions I give, than I ever see in the district. I think men stay up on teaching practices more than women. It's just my feeling.

*****

Mike: I go to a lot of workshops. There's so much coming out about teaching nowadays. It's hard to keep up. But it's important to.

Paul: Do all your peers feel the same as you do?

Mike [laughs]: Some do, but ... most of them ... this isn't going to sound nice, but I don't think the women stay on top of things as much. There seem to be more men at the workshops than women. Well, not more, but a greater proportion than are teaching in general.

By being a superlative teacher, it is possible to fend off potential suspicions since, presumably, it will be obvious that all of the interactions with the children are being properly channeled into the subject matter. This means that the men feel they have to perform at a higher level just to keep the same job, analogous to what women in predominantly male occupations must do.[26]

Men are inferior to their women peers in terms of their ability to openly nurture the children. This is not a trivial matter in the primary grades where nurturing is a major component of teaching. Early education is strongly associated with motherhood, and, as such, with physical contact and tender ministrations. While women teachers can safely and uncritically integrate these behaviors into their pedagogy as a means of transmission of curriculum content, men cannot.

The men find themselves in the awkward position of choosing among several alternatives. First, they can reject outright the notion of nurturing being important to children's learning and focus only on subject matter, thus reinforcing the perception that men bring a different style to the classroom. Second, they can defy all the proscriptions and get physically close to the children. In so doing, they risk the serious consequences already presented. Third, they can acknowledge that they can't get as close to children as the women teachers can and try to find other, compensatory, means to engage the children in learning in the absence of nurturing.

Thomas Gerschick and Adam Miller found a similar model that describes the relationship that men with disabilities have with hegemonic masculinity. They found that the disabled men could either "reject" traditional definitions of masculinity and create an alternative form, "rely" on traditional masculinity and judge themselves to be deficient, or "reformulate" hegemonic masculinity by defining it in terms of their specific capabilities.[27] Other researchers have concluded that men in predominately female occupations are similarly positioned. What is at stake, they contend, is the men's self-esteem and identity as men.[28]

In the case of teachers, however, it is not entirely clear which identity—man or teacher—they see as being under attack. It may be a combination of both, setting up a dizzying array of options through which the men must negotiate regularly yet inconsistently depending on the immediate situation.

The most immediate issue for men teachers appears to be to reconcile with the ambiguous demands of teaching. Since that obligation includes a tenuous relationship with hegemonic masculinity, I have chosen to center the teacher role within this model rather than masculinity itself. This marks a dramatic departure from what has been well received and accepted as an explanation for the scarcity of men in "women's occupations" by focusing on the structure of teaching rather than the psyches of the individual men.

Using the three-part model from above, I will present some examples of the ways the men negotiate their relationship with the conflict that is inherent in the situation where men are attempting to do what only "mothers" are seen as appropriate for doing.

Rejection Approach. Some of the men simply reject the idea of teachers needing to be surrogate mothers. Their approach is curriculum-oriented, and they state frankly that school is a place to learn. Two of the men, Dave and Dennis, fall into this category.

> Dave: As I said, I just don't think we should keep putting this image out of elementary school being a nursery. The kids start their education right in kindergarten, and the good teachers, men and women, focus on the basics. I can tell the kids that have been mothered instead of educated in the first couple years. They can't function at third-grade level.

> *****

> Dennis: There needs to be more emphasis on how the brain works. As teachers, we have to focus more on how the kids are learning and a little less on how they are feeling.

Even with this rejection stance, however, these men don't feel that a school should be a place without hugs and attention. They simply reject the notion that the success of the teachers depends on their tendency to "mother."

The remaining thirty-one teachers[29] do believe that nurturing behaviors are important to the overall ability of the children to learn. These men can be categorized by their activity in response to this belief. Five men are openly defiant of the touching rules and touch, hug, and get close to the children in the ways women teachers are thought to do. The remaining twenty-six men take some form of compensatory stance. Some said they realize that the children are likely missing something, but they felt they made up for that void in other ways, particularly by providing a "male role model," which was something the children wouldn't get in women teachers' rooms. The remainder cited very specific actions or activities by which they compensated for their lack of intimacy.

Defiance Approach. As presented earlier, ignoring the occupational mandates that dictate men's distancing themselves from children can be disastrous for the transgressor. Even so, several of the men I interviewed have decided to go forward with their intentions of interacting with the children exactly the way they feel the children need them to do and the way that will produce conditions most conducive to learning. That is, the men are teaching the way they see their women peers teaching, including freely touching and nurturing the children. Along with Roger and Keith, presented earlier, John also sees it as important to the children to provide a loving, supportive, and physically close relationship. These three men are among those who virtually ignore the rules regarding physical contact. It is clear that these men have internalized the model of teacher as nurturer and are demonstrating the behaviors associated with this model.

> John: I think I get as many hugs as Mary [his teaching partner] does! Yeah, I do. In fact, lately, my kids have been doing something—we'll be cleaning up and coming up to the rug, and they'll come up, and they'll like line up and give me a bunch of hugs and run around and sit down. They do that a lot; one kid does something and then they all do something.

> Paul: And, no problem with the hugs, huh?

> John: No, no. Kindergarten teachers get more hugs than any other grade level.

Compensatory Approach. Eighteen of the men told me that they felt they compensated for the lack of "mothering," in their classrooms. Bill and Don are examples of men who apparently feel nurturing is important, but they can't risk being demonstrative so they acknowledge a deficiency that is compensated for in other areas. Like the men in the Gerschick and Miller study of disabled men, they feel incapable of living up to the standard set. They do not present any specific behaviors that are intended to operate in the place of nurturing, however. Instead, they simply feel that they are giving their students the "other side" of teaching, the male role model, which students in women's classrooms miss.[30]

> Bill: Well, there's disadvantages and advantages. The disadvantage is that I'm not going to be able to be as affectionate with them. It's not that I can't. It's just, as I said before, society just won't allow it at this time. The advantage is that they do get the maleness from me.

*****

> Don: I see them getting real close to the teacher next door. They can't wait to hold onto her and hug her. Sometimes that gets to me. I mean, I can't be that for them, but there are other things they get from me.

> Paul: For example?

> Don: Well, they get a male.

In going back over the transcripts from the interviews and focus groups, I was able to identify the men who specifically use compensatory activities to strategically attempt to offset the lack of touching and closeness in their classrooms. There are several clusters of these techniques, which I've organized under the labels "greetings," "kudos," and "comforters."

Greetings. "High Fives" and handshakes are the most common form of greeting between the teachers and the children. This might not seem remarkable except that many of the men have gone to great lengths to institutionalize the exchange, thus removing the danger of any spontaneous physical contact, much like men in bureaucratized organizations and the "closeness without intimacy" players in organized sports.[31]

Larry: I do this thing in the morning when I come in when they're all lined up on the side, in two lines, before they come in. I do the thing I call HHH. They can either give me a hug, a handshake, or a high five depending on their comfort level, so I can have some sort of "hey, good morning" or just to have some kind of a bond, so they don't just come in and it's like, "good morning" and you never have any real interaction.[32]

*****

Howard: It's great just to have them line up for high fives. I go around the room and check on what they're doing in each group, and as soon as they see me making my rounds, they know it's time to high five.

Kudos. When the children are to be acknowledged for doing a good job, material rewards and verbal praise are used extensively as forms of kudos. As with the greetings above, there would be little that is remarkable about such behaviors except that these techniques are used in lieu of, rather than in addition to, things such as touching, hugging, and sitting on the teacher's lap.

Allen: I think there's a certain age that I feel uncomfortable with that [physical contact]. I do think that a child needs to know that you care in lots of ways instead of ... I do have my little rewards area and things like that, the treasure chest with every piece of junk in the world in it.

*****

Frank: But I think it makes me teach differently. You know, I'm always jumpy around the kids. Hey these kids are still little. They need a little hug and they need a little nurturing when they've done

something well. At least writing their names on one
of the boards gives them some positive feedback in
my room.

Comforters. When children need a bit of comforting, the men
who use compensatory activities find ingenious ways to provide it.
Dennis, one of the men who frankly denied the importance of
"mothering" to learning, also told me he substitutes for cuddling in
times of need.

> Dennis: I can't do what a female does—greater
> contact. I try to sit in a chair, for instance, and have
> them come up to me, and they'll sit in the chair
> next to me, and I'll pat them on the back. You
> know, you can get away with the attaboys or pat-
> ting them on the head and do those kind of things,
> but to actually sit them on your lap and do those....
> Very, very rarely will that happen unless the child
> is like, you know, their mother's just walked away
> and they're really scared and they're breaking
> down crying. Well, then you need, there's a little
> bit more contact it seems to me needed by the
> child. Just to let them know that everything's fine
> and, you know, to make sure that their breathing is
> getting right. I really work on their breathing when
> they get nervous or ... I say, "Let's take a deep
> breath and relax," and it's hard for them to cry a lot
> if they're taking deep breaths and holding it.

It is clear that the men in this study expend much of their energy
to avoid situations that could be interpreted negatively. Their presentations of these compensatory activities were at first quite positive, even exuberant in tone. As the interviews progressed, however,
their tone and choice of words revealed strong displeasure, often
anger. This was especially clear in the focus groups, as I discussed
in the previous section.

The dramatic change that took place in the tone of the men's presentation of these issues deserves considerable discussion. Other researchers have also encountered presentations similar to those that arose early in my study. Taken alone, these optimistic statements would indicate that the men are thriving on their uniqueness. If we define their situation in terms of a kind of "happy minority," we are in danger of overlooking some important institutionalized practices and assumptions that work against men fully integrating into the elementary school culture. The works of Rosemary Pringle, Myra Strober and David Tyack, and Christine Williams all seem to reflect a kind of "feel good" atmosphere in which the men admit to some difficulties but basically enjoy many privileges similar to those available to them from the larger patriarchal system. In addition, there is the sense that the men teaching elementary school are "just passing through" and so do not suffer any long-term effects from any differential treatment they receive while employed in "women's work."[33]

Had the issue of scrutiny not emerged and the men's negative reactions to it not become crystal clear in the focus groups, I might have been tempted to interpret much of what the men told me through a veil of optimism like that which informed much of the work regarding women preparing themselves to enter male-dominated occupations in the 1970s. According to much of that literature, it was the psyche of the individual woman, not the organizational culture and structure, that was problematized.[34] This smacked of blaming the victim and was quickly criticized by feminist scholars such as Rosabeth Moss Kanter.[35] Viewed through a prism of increased scrutiny, however, many of the seemingly trivial events in these men's lives loom large.

In summary, the emphasis in primary teaching is on the nurturing of the individual with substantive material being introduced in the process. The teacher must "be there" for the student.[36] Jennifer Nias describes primary teaching as requiring teaching that arises from personal values, especially from an ethic of caring. The process of teaching at the primary grades is one that builds and maintains close relationships.[37] Primary teaching is conceptualized, if not explicitly then surely implicitly, as an extension of "mothering." As

Barbara Risman points out, if all else is equal, one would expect men to mother the same as women. But all else is far from equal. In just this one major issue alone, the expectations of the school and society regarding physical contact with children, men experience a dramatically different set of "microstructural conditions" than do their women peers.[38]

James King suggests that we may be openly recruiting men into teaching while covertly sabotaging them through scrutinizing those who are not married or those who "act funny."[39] This scrutiny contributes to the men's adopting "safe" behaviors around the children that may be seen as antithetical to the children's needs. This becomes a self-fulfilling prophecy as the men retreat into behavior patterns that are stereotypically masculine and clearly contradictory to our perception of motherly behavior.

~ 4 ~

Elementary School: A Gendered World

Man for the field and woman for the hearth;
Man for the field and for the needle she;
Man with the head and woman with the heart;
Man to command and woman to obey;
All else confusion.

—From "The Princess"
by Alfred Lord Tennyson, 1847

In this chapter I will present a look into the gendered division of labor that exists at the men teachers' schools. To the best of my ability I have structured the presentation to reflect the order and form that our conversations took when I asked the men to tell me about "any ways your teaching experiences might differ from those of women teachers." It is safe to say that most of the men anticipated this question since my initial contact with each of them had explicitly revealed I was exploring the lived experiences of *men* teachers. My early interviews had not been particularly fruitful when I asked the men direct questions about what they were expected to do, or prevented from doing, *because* they were men. I could sense them pulling into themselves, becoming uncomfortable with the conversation, and generally avoiding answering. In looking over those early transcripts, I believe that the cause of their reticence was that any specific

answers that affirmed a division of labor could be read as an indict-
ment of their women peers rather than an analysis of the occupational
structure. By asking a more general question and then using strategic
prompts and probes, I arrived at the responses I'm presenting.

The men themselves see these points as being germane to a full
appreciation of their gendered lives. Of particular importance were
the sex of their principals, the tasks that are allocated to men and
women, their individual paths to teaching, the place of children in
their lives, and ways to increase the number of men in elementary
teaching.

The Principals

I found that twenty-four of the thirty-five men worked at
schools with women principals, a proportion slightly higher than
national figures.[1] Several men felt that the sex of the principal was
important in terms of the kind of work environment the principal
created or maintained. For example, several teachers, when speaking of the ways jobs are allocated among the staff, said that, since
the principal at their site is a woman, gender issues are likely to be
handled equitably.

> Eduardo: I don't think there's really any difference
> in the way jobs are assigned. Our principal, a
> woman, is ... she's pretty on top of things, and I
> don't think she really allows that kind of thing
> [gendered division of labor] to happen. I think
> she's pretty sharp in that area.

*****

> Frank: I think having a female principal kind of
> keeps things on an even keel in terms of how things
> get assigned. She's very alert to discrimination of
> all kinds.

*****

> Keith: My principal's a woman. I think they're
> more sensitive to issues such as treating people dif-
> ferently. As a gay man, I appreciate that.

Many of the men teachers see women principals as being more
fair, perhaps because as women they have experienced gender
oppression and therefore are more likely to recognize oppression in
other areas. On the other hand, Peggy McIntosh would assert that
women are likely to be blind to their own privileges, for example
those arising out of their whiteness, and require some additional
information beyond their own experiences to help them see the
oppression of others. She cites her exposure to the theoretical perspectives addressed in women's studies as the source of her critical
model that allows her to see the subtle indicators of "privilege."
Women's lived experiences, however, certainly provide them with a
frame to help them easily understand oppression in its many forms.[2]
Interestingly, none of the men I interviewed stated openly that
because their principal is a man the tasks are *unfairly* distributed.

Despite the possibility that women principals attend more to
issues of gender equity than men would, I have found that the division of labor at the teachers' school sites is clearly gendered and the
"culture" the men describe is not entirely friendly (see Chapter Six).

In addition to the principal's sex affecting task assignment,
other men simply made note of the majority of women in positions
of power.

> Eduardo: Sometimes I get teased, "Hey, Eduardo,
> when you gonna ... when you gonna become a prin-
> cipal." But I don't know where that comes from.
> I've never really indicated that that's what I want to
> do. I clearly don't want to do it. It's funny. This is
> my third school, and I've had a female principal in
> all the schools. Maybe I should start asking *them*.
> [laughs]

I will discuss more about the issue of men teachers becoming principals in another section. What we are seeing here is the relatively rare instance of women controlling the work of men. This control is direct in the cases where the principals are women. At every school, though, women indirectly control the work of men by being in the majority and thereby setting the pace and standards for the work.[3] Women themselves are so much in the majority that most don't see the school site as gendered at all.

Having a man as principal came into the conversation in only two ways. First was in the simple listing of the few other men who might work at the school. More important, the men told of the expectations that the women teachers had concerning the possible relationships between men teachers and their principals. The most prevalent idea was that men principals are likely to have a leadership style that is not conducive to cooperative interaction. Like Dennis, a kindergarten teacher, many of the men feel that the women at their schools expect the men to handle interactions that require assertiveness, especially if speaking with the principal is involved.

> If you have a male principal, he tends to dictate.
> Women tend to listen and sit back. They may bitch
> and everything about it, but they'll sit and listen,
> and if there's a complaint, they're expecting one of
> the male teachers to go complain to the male.

While Dennis' principal is a man, Fred (who teaches third grade) has a woman principal, and his narrative reveals the same notion of male assertiveness.

> Since they knew I was not hesitant to speak out on
> an issue, they would probably approach me and
> say, "Hey, would you bring this up at the faculty
> meeting? Would you mind bringing this up? I don't
> need Mary getting mad at me."

Of the nine teachers who told me that they felt their women

peers expected them to take the lead in negotiations with authoritative principals, seven have women principals. All of these men went on, like Chuck (first grade), to say that the expectation was not entirely desirable.

> I can't see me being the foot soldier, you know? I don't need the extra headache. Besides, there's no need to get upset about these things.

Yet, in spite of their misgivings, all of the men said that quite often they accept the task and speak to the principal as a representative of the other teachers. By acting in expected ways and approaching the principal, the men teachers are helping to reinforce perceived gender differences. Stereotypically, men are thought to be more assertive, task-oriented, utilitarian, and authoritarian. Most of the men in my study frankly reject these descriptions of themselves. Accepting the assignment of speaking to the principals may simply be a case of the men trying to redefine what they see as a negative characteristic (assertiveness in the context of teaching of small children) into a positive one in terms of peer relations.

Regarding the issue of the gender breakdown of the teachers, the men usually described a staff consisting of twenty-five to thirty women teachers with between two and four men. Many of the men could tell me the current as well as past gender proportions at their own as well as other schools. Considering the lack of communication among men from different sites (see Chapter Six), this is remarkable and demonstrates that they attend to this information closely.

> Javier: There is one other male teacher and um ... my last school, I think there were two other male teachers.

*****

> John: When I first came there were three male teachers and the principal was male, and then one

> male teacher went to be a school-based resource
> teacher at another school in the district. The other
> one transferred out this year, and our principal took
> another job in Pupil Services.

*****

> Jake: Up until this year I was the only male, dis-
> counting our principal and the custodian. I was the
> only teacher.

In about a third of the interviews, the men listed employees such as the custodian and gardener as part of the male population even though the context of the interview clearly called for teaching personnel. More understandably, they listed men resource specialists, bi-lingual specialists, and counselors, who comprise a significant proportion of the total male elementary teaching population. Between the men's descriptions and the information available in the directory I used for locating teachers, my sense is that men are "overrepresented" in these non-classroom positions when compared to the elementary teaching population in general. This is also true of the gender breakdown of principals. Since men are forty-eight percent of the general population, they are underrepresented as principals. They are arguably overrepresented as principals when compared to the teaching staff (thirty percent compared to twelve percent). One point that is not entirely clear is the occupational origin of elementary school principals. According to the men I interviewed and based on a national survey, many of the men principals come from backgrounds other than elementary school teaching.[4]

Division of Labor

Most of the teachers I interviewed enumerated several tasks that were performed more by one sex than the other. In many discussions, although the participants provided some rationale for the division of labor, they also described it in terms of impediments to their teaching. As I will discuss later under "culture," the men are hesitant to complain about this imbalance. Briefly stated, a refusal to perform in stereotypical ways increases general suspicion about a man. In addition, in some ways, refusal represents a failure on the part of the man to fulfill the male covenant in teaching. Some researchers have interpreted the assignment of gender-specific tasks as special treatment.

> This special treatment bothered some respondents. Getting assigned all the "discipline problems" can make for difficult working conditions, for example. But many men claimed this differential treatment did not cause distress. In fact, several said they liked being appreciated for the special traits and abilities (such as strength) they could contribute to their professions.[5]

Being asked to fix a tire is like being asked to make coffee. Neither is particularly harmful unless it is fashioned into a job as part of a structure of gendered differentiation. Neither qualifies as "special treatment." When one must behave in stereotypically gendered ways to retain a job, this cannot be considered preferential treatment. In fact, as I explained in Chapter Three, many of the stereotypical behaviors of men are actually compensatory activities designed to make up for institutionalized restrictions on men's intimate contact with the children.

Men are often asked to take on the physical tasks associated with teaching. Tasks such as lifting heavy objects, doing dirty or risky repairs, and even filling in for the custodian are all considered part of the man teacher's job. Non-teaching manual chores were high on the list of least desirable aspects of being a man teacher.[6]

> Eduardo [who felt that the woman principal at his school kept gendered division of labor to a minimum]: Oh, occasionally I'll be asked to lift something, something like that, but you know, that's only natural. I mean they're going to ask the

strongest person. Of course, they assume I'm strong. I'm not entirely sure they're right. Some of the stuff I'm sure they could just as easily lift. I'm not saying they go out of their way to come and get me to do work, but....

In addition, men are often expected to have technical knowledge that allows them to maintain almost anything and so find themselves responsible for school equipment.

George: Amazingly, all the heavy stuff is stored in my room.

Paul: What kind of stuff?

George: Video equipment, portable screens, trunks with project materials, volleyball poles, miscellaneous junk.

Paul: Why is it all in your room? Was it there when you started teaching?

George: No, and I've changed rooms twice. The stuff just follows me. Whenever anyone needs heavy things set up, I get a little note in my box to bring it to room such-'n'-such.

Paul: Have you ever spoken with any one about this?

George: I brought it up once, and the principal just dismissed it as whining. I got the impression that I was supposed to feel special, needed.

Many of the men uncritically see assignment to stereotypical tasks as simple, courteous requests, as with Bill.

> Bill: I don't think that there's anything I'm
> expected to do because I'm a male. I don't know.
> Can I change the question a little bit? If the ques-
> tion was "are there things that I'm *asked* to do
> because I'm a male," then I think that there are
> some things. For example, this morning I was
> asked to climb a ladder to put some things up in a
> classroom, and I think that was partially because I
> was a male. Similar things that males would tradi-
> tionally do around the school. Not expected.

However, most of the men were far more likely to relate stories
like the following:

> Javier: Of course, they will ask me to move things
> and lift stuff. I probably get more than my share of
> … oh, I don't know, the unruly boys. When I
> taught fifth grade there was probably more of that.
> I don't get the idea that the school puts too many
> difficult third graders in my class. Maybe occa-
> sionally.

The issue of "unruly boys" was addressed by most of the men
and will be discussed below. Manuel's response is typical of the
kinds of lists that the men verbally checked off for me regarding the
distribution of duties and of the way that verbalizing one activity
reminded them of other tasks.

> Manuel: So other than that, I don't think anything's
> delegated differently to males or females. Just
> those manual labor tasks that come throughout the
> day. Other than that there's nothing else. Oh, social
> committee. That's usually always females. That's
> the one that plans all the parties and stuff for the
> staff. It's usually almost always female. And then
> see the technology is usually always male, now

that you mentioned it. [I didn't—he did.] Usually all the males are on the technology committees. A lot of the women say, "Oh, I can't do the technology, I can't do the VCR, I can't do this. High tech, that's your guys' area." That's a large group of males with maybe a few females on the technology committee, where the social committee, that's more of a ... so those two types of tasks, which still help run the school are run by.... So I think that's portrayed in society too. All those stereotypical roles. Women are better at planning parties, and men are better at fixing machines. I don't believe that way, but that's what is portrayed at our school. Plus males get the harder children a lot of times. The behavior problems will usually be in our classes. Like I said, you're there to get that discipline in, because you're a disciplinarian. They're going to listen to you better than to anyone else. So a lot of teachers, consciously or unconsciously, they put tough kids in our classrooms. So we always have a lot of behavior problems initially. If there's heavy boxes downstairs the males always carry them up to the other teachers, so stuff that comes in the mail, book orders and stuff. If an assembly has to be set up quickly, it's usually the males that are moving furniture, setting up chairs, like those types of tasks are part of your teaching day.

Most of the men began by saying that there is very little in the way of a gendered division of labor. As they talked, however, they continued to add more tasks to their lists. That is, they remembered more tasks, obligations, and expectations that are associated with gender. This has led me to use the phrase "absent presence" when describing gender in the men's lives. It's there, but lies invisible to immediate consciousness.[7] This is especially obvious in Manuel's comment, "now that *you* mention it." Not one of the men ever ended by acknowledging that the list he presented does, in fact, confirm the presence of a gendered division of labor. Furthermore, these men all stated that they did not "dare" to protest the situation. While this point will be discussed in detail in Chapter Six, Javier's response is informative since he is consistent with others.

> I certainly can't ... I wouldn't complain to them about carrying things, moving stuff, I mean ... you know, it's kind of hard enough as it is.

Often, performing physical tasks is viewed as more of an individual choice rather than a product of gender structure. The idea that the men are choosing to take on stereotypical tasks and responsibilities is a dubious one since, whenever any group is confined to a narrow set of options out of a wide range of possibilities, personal choice cannot adequately explain actions.

> Robert: It's just less hassle, easier all around, to go ahead and go along with it [leaving his class when asked to do a physical chore].

In addition to strength issues, men are frequently expected to be the disciplinarians on campus and find that they have a disproportionate number of "problem" students, usually boys, in their classrooms. Bill and Howard tell similar stories.

> Bill: I think that there have been, at this school anyway. I feel like I've been given more difficult children, behaviorally, because I feel that feelings about me at school are that I'll deal with them and I won't give up on them and because I'm a male, I'll be more effective with them. I don't have anything to prove that, but I sense it because of the kids I've received and the class make-up I've received as compared to other class make-ups. So, I feel that that is a different expectation because I'm a male.

Bill is the teacher who modified my questions regarding gendered tasks from "expected to" to "asked to." While he may not have empirical evidence supporting his perception that men get the more difficult kids, Howard clearly has.

> Whenever a kid comes along who's more trouble-some than usual, either Frank or I are asked to have him in our class. I asked the principal once why she wanted to put a particular kid in my room and she told me he would push a female teacher around. These kids are only eight. I told her I didn't really look forward to a career as a warden. She told me to get used to it because it is accepted practice to have male teachers handle aggressive kids.

The men "get used to" many of the issues discussed in these narratives and thereby come to see them as "accepted practice." Boys appear to be the unruly kids more than girls, and teachers like Roger seem to take pride in their ability to deal with them.

> I've never felt that somebody thought that I should-n't be teaching young children because I'm a man. Never. Either from staff, students or parents, never, never heard it. In fact, I think they really appreci-ate it, especially administrators. Because they are locked into that thing, too. "You're a man, this is a young man, this is a boy that's, you know, kind of high energy, you know, attention-deficit, he needs that male." And I think that they tend to focus and send students to you accordingly at times, which I welcome. I enjoy working with the, you know, with those boys who kind of drive the other teach-ers crazy [laughs]. I'm kind of the special place-ment room. I get a lot of special, special kids.

Don, a first-grade teacher who had only been teaching a little more than a year, revealed how imbedded this practice is. In response to my general query about gendered differential experiences, he replied:

> No, none. I don't think so. No, I don't think I get any kids, say, with behavioral problems. At least that hasn't happened yet. That's not to say it won't, I guess.
>
> Paul: Why did you pick that particular subject—difficult students?
>
> Don: Well, I mean, because, uh, I think that it might happen. I think that it does happen because maybe there's a perception out there that male teachers are like more of a disciplinarian.

Being assigned unruly students can create more problems for men. They will have to focus more on discipline in their classrooms. This may influence the climate in men's classes to the point that they are, in fact, more likely to come across as disciplinarians, a classic case of the self-fulfilling prophecy. The structure of the elementary school gender order assigns disciplinary tasks to those who are expected to be most qualified to perform them. Traditionally men have been associated with the disciplining of children in families and schools as well as associated with task- and goal-orientation.[8] As Dave tells us, the prevailing image of men teachers may not resonate well with the men's self-definitions.

> You know, so they say, "oh, he needs a good role model," or "he needs a strong hand," or something like that. Thinking that since I'm male, I'm going to have a stronger hand, which is not necessarily true.

While the men are being steered toward discipline, they are also being directed away from nurturing. Although I discussed this in more detail when I presented the men's reaction to being under close scrutiny, this is also important in other, more day-to-day functions, as in the case of Barry, a first-grade teacher.

> I had the strangest thing happen to me. I had a little girl who was getting picked on until she broke down and cried. I took her aside and wiped her tears and talked to her for a while until she felt better. Later in the day, one of the other teachers came in and asked me about the girl. When I told her what happened, she told me she had better take the girl out and talk to her to make sure she was O.K. I was REALLY insulted by that. She wouldn't have gone into a female teacher's classroom and taken the girl out. I wish I had told her to mind her own business, but I didn't dare. I feel like any special relationship that the girl and I had is shot.

Fred, a third-grade teacher, related a story to me of a time when one of his previous students, who had moved up to sixth grade, came by to see him and tried to give him a hug. Fred felt he had perhaps been overly zealous in rejecting her attempts at physical contact, so he asked a woman teacher to seek out the student and comfort her.

> So I asked her, "Will you take Christine aside and tell her, 'Fred still likes you, Fred still thinks you're great, but you know it might be inappropriate.'"

The task of comforting students appears to fall into the domain of women teachers. Mike, like Barry (above), is offended by this proscription but, as with all the men, is not prepared to complain.

> It just irks me that my duties are limited by my sex. I'm perfectly willing to take my turn watching over

> the athletic field [supervising the large area where boys play], but once in a while I'd like to be in contact with the girls and learning more about how they interact. It's important to me as a teacher to relate to the students a lot of different ways.

In a typical school day, men elementary school teachers appear to be doing exactly what women elementary school teachers are doing: educating children. However, there are assumptions embedded in the culture of elementary schools that influence men and women into different recesses of the job. Some of these influences are subtle, some overt. Although most of the men are concerned with the differential treatment, they tend to see it as a result of the application of accepted notions of gender difference, even when they, personally, do not buy into the gender difference as natural. Those who are annoyed most are willing to tell me that they are unhappy with the restrictions imposed but say that any protest on their part would exacerbate the problem and add more difficulty to their work lives. While some may argue that the men themselves are often complicit in this gendered arrangement, the negative sanctions that, according to the men, would befall them if they did not accept the responsibilities, or even if they questioned the traditions, make the notion of complicity a *non sequitur*. When I asked Adam, a second-grade teacher, about the contradictory expectations in his workday, he told me, echoing Javier above, that he just accepted it as part of the job, rather than protesting and causing further difficulties for himself.

> I don't really talk about that because any time you share an opinion that they don't like, they say, "well, that's the male perspective," or they have some little thing like that so there's really no point in letting them know that you don't like doing something. It'll just make it worse.

Career Paths

The topic of "getting into teaching" arose in every interview as the men recounted events and choices in their lives that they felt best explained their journeys. Some stressed the influence of a significant person in their lives or a major event that showed them the appropriateness or appeal of teaching. Others recounted a rational decision about the pay, benefits, time off, and continuity with other life activities offered by teaching. Their future plans seldom included anything but continued teaching, yet they told me they often receive hints that perhaps they should be thinking about moving into domains more appropriate for men. Most striking for me was the ways in which the men wove events with children, especially their own, into these narratives.

Several teachers told me of the influence of significant people in their lives that led to their choosing teaching as an occupation. Not surprising, some of them named a man teacher.

> Don: I don't want to sound like a cliché, but I had a very good teacher in fifth grade. He was very instrumental. My dad was not home at the time a lot. More or less he was like a father figure. I'm not sure, but I think it had something to do with it. In college I changed my major quite a few times and then I went into education. When I was doing my student teaching, I knew that I had made the right choice. I enjoyed it.

*****

> Norman: I was heavily influenced by my father, who was an elementary school teacher. So I do have fond memories of going to the classroom with him as a child and watching him teach, which was interesting. The first time I saw my father in front of a group of kids teaching [he exhibited] a little different personality. So at that point I figured, am

I going to be a waiter all my life, or am I going to
go back to school and do something?

Teaching as a career choice was often a result of the men measuring the economic and social costs and benefits of the occupation
against their personal goals. Frequently they questioned the stereotypical masculine criteria for success.

> Dennis: But there's this idea that you come out of
> the university and you're a teacher, and thirty years
> later you're a teacher, somehow that in a male psy-
> che is not supposed to be right. It means somehow
> you aren't successful and you need to move up.

*****

> Dave: I think a lot of men have the idea that you're
> not going to make any money teaching elementary
> school. I'm very comfortable. I give a lot of money
> to charity. I live in this house. I got a pool. I mean,
> what do you want? You know, you can only eat so
> many steaks at each meal as they say. Some might
> question my sense of responsibility for not having
> a real job.

Men teachers frequently receive unsolicited allusions to their
appropriateness for administrative positions, special teaching
assignments, or teaching at higher-grade levels. This "tracking" happens, in one form or another, in all phases of the men's careers,
including during teacher training. Here I only want to give voice to
Allen and Dwight and follow up in other sections.

> Allen: I take college courses in art, music, and
> other subjects just to round myself out for the kids.
> I'm always learning something new to bring in and
> have fun with. The story around the school is that I
> must be trying to get promoted by taking more

units. I can't believe that they won't accept the fact
I just love teaching.

*****

Dwight: The district office and the county send out
employment opportunity flyers whenever there's an
open position for guidance or something. It seems
they never forget to mention to the men when there's
an opening. It's like we probably don't really like
teaching and can hardly wait to get out. It almost
feels like they're saying we should get out.

There is a widely accepted theory that men teachers can align
with men principals and administrators because of their maleness
and seek promotions to administrative positions. In this way they
enjoy a hidden advantage by being "tracked into better paying, more
prestigious specialties." [9] This theory relies on a model of the occupation that is negated by the evidence in these interviews. The model
that underlies this theory, as expressed by Christine Williams, displays an occupation many men enter for the express purpose of
attaining administrative positions.

In some cases, men were told by recruiters there
were special advancement opportunities for men in
these fields, and they entered them expecting rapid
promotion to administrative positions. [10]

Williams' model includes other more ambivalent men, who ultimately choose to conform to dominant definitions of masculine success and seek more power, prestige, and remuneration. Still others
find it is too difficult to "resolve internal conflicts involving their masculinity." [11] People *outside* the profession might stigmatize the men
for remaining with the children. In addition, this model suggests that
men teachers who form allegiances with their women peers may run
the risk of being seen as deviants (unreliable, homosexual, pedophile)
by men administrators. All of these contribute to the tendency of men

teachers to seek or accept promotions, usually through the teachers' relationships with men principals.[12] According to Williams:

> A major difference in men and women in nontraditional occupations is that men in these situations are far more likely to be supervised by a member of their own sex.[13]

My research reveals several problems with this composite model. First, getting promoted to principal is clearly not an important objective to the men I interviewed. Second, a point that I will demonstrate throughout this research, the major source of conflict that the men face regarding their masculinity is not internal to themselves but resides in the institutionalized expectations that are ambiguous, even contradictory, and force them to teach differently from the women around them. The major task for the men is to avoid any accusations of molestation, and the key actors who monitor the men's activities and who could generate suspicions are *within* the men's occupational sphere, not outside of it. Third, the demographics simply do not support the notion of men's supposed "fast track" into administration. The percentage of women elementary school principals has been increasing dramatically for the past twenty years.[14]

Most of the men see principalship as an entirely different job category from teaching. Andrew Cognard-Black has demonstrated that men's attrition rate from elementary teaching is not greater than women's and that men move "out" of the occupation (quit teaching) and move "over" (to non-classroom positions), more than they move "up" into administration.[15] In addition, the National Association of Elementary School Principals present data that show men elementary principals come out of other career positions, for example secondary teaching, more often than from elementary teaching.[16]

Almost all of the men stated frankly that they expected to be teaching into the distant future. Many were open about their choice of alternative notions of what defines success. Power and high earning potential were not motivational factors that figured into their career choice. Kindergarten teacher Norman's narrative is an amalgam of many teachers' thoughts about the difference between teaching and being a principal.

> I wouldn't be interested in being a principal. I get joy from being with the kids, and as far I can see right now, that would not be something that I would want to do. Every once in a while a parent will say something like, "We would really like to have you as a principal." My response has been that it's a nice compliment—at least that's what it is to me. But I always say that my joy is here with the kids. And, also, from my point of view, being in the culture of elementary education, the motivations for being a teacher and being a principal are night and day. A principal is not like the same job. I think that that might be how, unfortunately, it's being perceived, that being a principal is just a step up but still really the same thing as teaching, and it's a totally different ball game—at least the way I see it.

While teachers like Eduardo and Norman were relatively open with me in their rejection of dominant forms of masculine success, it was clear that they were not in the habit of disclosing these thoughts and feelings at work.

> Eduardo: I always feel like they're looking at me funny when I say I'd just as soon keep teaching rather than move up. It's like I'm not doing what a man's supposed to do.

> *****

> Norman: It's just assumed that a man's gonna want to advance, but I came to teach and I want to keep teaching. Some of them really don't understand that. I mean, I can see it in their faces, like, "What's wrong with this guy?"

Mike, a teacher who takes great pride and joy in being his own children's primary parent, seemed to sum up this point:

> My wife works as an engineer in a management position and makes twice as much money as I do. So our whole role in society is turned around. And our role has been questioned by many of my friends at work. And just straight out, "Doesn't Mike feel bad about not making as much money as you do?" Like that really makes a difference to me. And who cares who makes the most money? I mean, what's the deal here, is this some competition? Have I got some sort of male ego that I can't deal with that?

Children in the Narratives

When I asked the men to tell me about early experiences with children, a few, like Jake, said they had had the opportunity to regularly care for children prior to teaching.

> Yeah, I was in charge of them [younger siblings] a lot because my mother worked and my father worked. So I did do a lot of baby-sitting, that kind of thing. I didn't especially like it, being a teenager. I could think of better things to do with my time.

Most of the men, however, told me they did not have much contact with small children before becoming teachers. Almost all, however, reported that they had become involved in some sort of children-oriented activity at the point in their lives when the decision to teach was made. Examples include working at a summer camp, volunteering at a boys' and girls' club, participating in after-school programs, and tutoring. I had brought with me the preconceived notion that what I was hearing was a description of the moment in which they realized that children weren't so bad. But as I listened carefully, I heard something else. I also heard, in many cases, that they realized they weren't bad for children. At the least, they indicated that in their early lives they had assumed that they might hurt children, by dropping them, scaring them, or not nurturing them enough to meet their needs.

> Dennis: Oh, it [past experience with children] was very good. I was always pretty good with ... babies, you mean? Let's say I was okay with kids three or four years old. I was always okay. Younger than that, I was kind of afraid of them, afraid I was going to drop them, or something.

As I read remarks like these, I felt conflicting sensations. On the one hand, they were revelations in that they allowed me to see for the first time that, in terms of relations with children, the turning point in men's lives may not be when we find out that children are not mysterious creatures best left to the natural skills of women but instead it may be when the revolutionary notion is conceived that we are not inadequate in caring for them or harmful to them.

At the same time, I knew I had heard something similar to the idea of men being dangers to children before, but where? The answer emerged during an all-night grading session just a year or so ago. I teach several large "Sociology of Gender" classes each year at my university. The major requirement is to work at the Campus Children's Center, actively participating in activities with the children. After keeping an ethnographic record of their experiences, the students then write a paper in which they integrate their experiences with the literature of the class. That is, they compare the ideas of various authors regarding the maintenance of gender difference and inequality with what they observed at the center. I encourage my students to enrich their papers with any personal perspectives or outside sources that they feel will help convey their ideas.

As I was reading a particularly engaging paper, I was struck by the following passage:

> I was really scared of going to the Children's
> Center. The day we took the tour for orientation
> and I saw all those little kids, I just didn't think I
> was going to be able to do this project. What if I
> hurt one of them? I'd never been allowed to hold
> my little sister or any of my nieces or nephews. My
> sister did the baby-sitting even though she's three
> years younger than me.

The words "never been allowed" were like a wake-up call. I
read them several times, I think, before promising myself to review
all the past papers for this theme. I found myself privately embar-
rassed over the possibility that I perhaps had missed such an important point, especially one that was so pertinent to my study.

At the time of this writing, I have read over 1,400 of these
papers. Men wrote almost 500 of them, or thirty-five percent. Many
of the students included a statement in which they expressed some
apprehension over working at the center because of a lack of previous experiences with children.

> The idea of working with a large group of little kids
> really scared me. Up until now children have been a
> mystery for me. I was hoping to get out of the proj-
> ect because I don't know anything about children.

The proportion of men who made such statements was slightly
greater than of women who did. Taken alone, this is not particularly
surprising. What was significant, however, was that many of the
men described their apprehension in terms of the potential harm that
might befall the children at their hands.

Among the more mundane kinds of issues like, "I feel really big
and clumsy around them," "I'm afraid I might step on one of them,"
and "I was worried they might run and hide and not do anything
while I was around," were more serious concerns.

The teacher I reported to asked me to go to the room [where the toddlers are]. I almost threw up. I was so worried about hurting the little ones.

*****

What am I supposed to do? What's safe?

Also, even here, the specter of scrutiny raised its ugly head.

What if one of the parents comes to pick their kid up and sees me holding him?

*****

I started rubbing this girl's back to help her fall asleep, and it just felt like everyone was staring at me to see what I was going to do.

Not one woman wrote statements like these in her paper. However, both men and women frequently mentioned the lack of men at the center. Often the men wrote of being "the only man."

Returning to the men teachers, it is clear from the interviews with the teachers that the men's own children are very important to them and influence the way they teach—often even what grade they teach. Most important, they talk about their kids freely and persistently.

Roger: The young ones are the best. Hey, they're just, they're great. These kids are so cool. I would worry about teaching secondary. I would, very much so. It's a lot tougher to change a kid, or assist a kid in going down the right path, you know, in those teen years. I know; I'm a father. It's tough; it's tough. People, they say, "Teaching hard?" I say, no, my, the hard part of my day starts when I go home.

For most of the men with children, their lives appear to have a sense of coherence and continuity through the opportunity to be the same kind of person at work and at home. In addition, classroom experiences help them understand their own children and vice versa, as with Chuck:

> Oh, I think I'm very, very nurturing. If I see a child that's experiencing frustration or something, something that's going on at home, I'm real open to "if you don't feel good right now, why don't you just rest?" Because these kids take so much baggage to school. One problem on the page, what does it matter if they don't do it? I'm more concerned with their emotional well-being. I don't look just to educate the mind, but also the heart. I want to turn these kids into good people, you know? There's so much into reading techniques, math techniques, but I don't think they're addressing the whole child. And also, having a child now, my son's seven and a half months, it's also changing me a lot, made me much more empathetic.

As I presented in Chapter Three, however, the men with children may also experience a considerable amount of dissonance because their activities with children at school are inhibited by institutionalized policies and practices designed to protect the children from harm. They cannot be as nurturing with their students as they can with their own children, and often they catch themselves behaving in parental ways, which are considered unacceptable for men.

An Alternative Model

By focusing on psychological factors and factors that might pull at men's preference for positions of power and prestige, it is possible to overlook important factors embedded in the occupational and workplace cultures that push men out of teaching, particularly the disparate enforcement of touching rules, the overall scrutiny under which they must perform, and the difficulties they encounter in trying to nurture the children in their charge.

By listening carefully to the men, accepting that they may not feel individually powerful enough to surmount the institutional obstacles they face, and valuing their standpoint on these and other issues, we can position ourselves to contribute to a destabilization of the societal division of labor in new ways.[17] Several scholars have suggested that the low participation of men in elementary teaching must be explained using dramatically different approaches from those that are used to explain the low participation of women in male-dominated occupations. Some, like Christine Williams, frankly dismiss any reason for looking for solutions inside the structure and practices of the occupation itself.[18]

> Policies intended to alter the sex composition of male-dominated occupations—such as affirmative action—make little sense when applied to the "female professions." For men, the major barriers to integration have little to do with their treatment once they enter these fields.[19]

However, by focusing on the experiences of the men teachers and validating their expressions of anxiety, fear, and even anger over their contradictory positions, the analogy between their situation and that of women in male-dominated occupations becomes more reasonable. More important, many of the steps that have been taken to increase women's participation in "men's work" can also be seen as applicable, with some modification, to increasing men's participation in women's work.

> I'll tell you one thing, definitely, is that at school sites you have to have a certain number of Latinos. You gotta have a certain number of African Americans. The most underrepresented minority are men. Categorize men as a minority. It could be done; should be done. (Chuck, a first-grade teacher)

More Men Teachers

Jim Allan tells us there is a preference for hiring men on the part of some schools. He says this preferential hiring has three bases: a commitment to affirmative action, a desire on the part of men principals for male companionship, and the public's demand for more male models in the classroom.[20] None of the teachers I interviewed fully agreed with this assessment. Although many of them told me that they had heard many positive things from the teaching community and the public about how good it is to have male role models, their lived experiences leave them with the reality that there has been no significant increase in the number of men in primary teaching. While most of the men I interviewed confirmed that they have certainly encountered positive and optimistic rhetoric from administrators regarding some form of affirmative action, they could not recount any instances where the result was more men being hired. The idea that men principals would prefer to hire men in order to enjoy male companionship did not resonate well with most of these teachers' experiences. First, most of these men were hired by schools with women principals. Second, over half the men whose principals were men denied any real contact with the principal and believed that the principals came from a secondary school background rather than elementary school. Most of my participants saw principalship as being an entirely different occupational area from teaching and were more likely to view the teacher-administrator relationship in employee-employer terms rather than as a friendship or mentorship arrangement. None of the participants named the principal as their mentor, but instead identified another teacher, usually a woman.

When I asked the men in my project to tell me how they would go about increasing the number of men in teaching, I was surprised to find that four felt it would be a mistake to actively do so. Their concern was that any attempt to bring more men into the field would necessarily tap into a population of men who would be detrimental to teaching in general and the condition of men in particular. In sum, these men felt that a kind of self-selection is already taking place and providing the profession with only those men who are clearly cut out to teach. These men were quick to point out that this apprehension was not confined to men, but that any program that creates a wave of hiring brings inferior teachers into the profession. They did feel, however, that one problem specific to hiring more men was the increased likelihood of hiring men who might molest children.

Nevertheless, most of the participants stated that increasing the number of men is a worthwhile project, and all but five were very excited about the prospect. Their ideas fell into four specific themes, and most of the men mentioned more than one way to accomplish the task. Some listed all four, though not in identical order of priority.

First, they all suggested that increasing the pay of the occupation would have the effect of drawing some men in. None of the men felt that increasing pay was in itself sufficient, however. Two felt it would be a necessary modification in conjunction with other changes. Most of the men added that increasing teachers' pay would also help the profession compete with others in attracting high-achieving women. Second, nearly all of the men mentioned the need to change the image of teaching from that of "women's work." Third, almost half suggested that some changes need to be made in teacher education. Finally, the most often mentioned primary mechanism for change was some form of outreach. They felt that the way to increase the number of men in teaching is to introduce more males to the lived experiences of current men teachers.

Keith, a first-grade teacher, is representative of the men who suggested pay as a mechanism for increasing the number of men. As he spoke, his emphasis shifted from pay to outreach activities and then to the general issue of gender socialization.

> Uh, I think probably the quickest and easiest way that you could get males into education is [chuckle], well, pay them as much as you pay an accountant or somebody with an MBA. [Later, regarding high school curriculum]: Something like that, that is a parenting component where they, you know, they get some awareness of what it's like to be a parent.

So that those who find that they have the proclivity to really want to work with children, um, can learn so early, early on. 'Cause we encourage it in girls. Oh girls, oh yeah, they baby-sat, they became camp counselors, they've taught Sunday school. Guys, what have you done? Oh yeah, well I was on the football team. We've separated them early on. We've got to change the way we socialize kids.

The topic of pay entered the conversations in more than one way. In addition to the more typical, expected issue of increasing pay, some of the men talked about the idea that perhaps the pay is adequate but that the *perception* of the pay of the occupation is inaccurate. The false image, they contend, is that teaching produces paupers in the worst case and inadequate breadwinners at best.

John: I don't know, it's hard to say. Well, you can't really say, well, the money is great, you'll get rich teaching elementary school. I mean, you get by and you have benefits and a pension, but I mean it's ... you know, most of the dads driving up here are driving nicer cars than I am.

*****

Dennis: I've talked to superintendents who came up with the idea that teaching pay was designed for women who went to college and became a professional as a teacher, but they were the second income in the family and not the primary and so the pay has been that way for years and that's why.

Aside from pay issues, the other three actions closely resemble the affirmative action and equal opportunity proposals designed to assist women and men of color to enter white- and/or male-dominated occupations.

The predominant image of teaching is that it is women's work.

This theme pervades almost all the conversations I've had with men teachers, regardless of the specific topic under discussion. The allusion is not to demographics, but to the perceptions and constructions associated with the work that exclude men as typical workers.

> Javier: Probably the first thing would be to get the word out that this is not just for women.

> Paul: Could you explain "getting the word out?"

> Javier: Well, basically change the image I guess. You know, the general image is that teaching little kids is something that you need a woman for, a mother for, that the little kids need mothering and nurturing more than they need education. But that's just not true. All elementary school teachers, men and women, take the education of these children quite seriously. We need to show more men doing it. Men can be very nurturing, and we may not demonstrate it like women do. I just think that when you see pictures of little children in school, I just think that they could show more men doing it.

The need for changing the image of teaching is closely linked to the need for improving the overall image of men as they relate with children.

> Eduardo: We need more images of men with little children. It's getting a little better. You know, we're seeing more ads where Dad is taking care of the baby and such. But most of the time the message is that Dad's incompetent, that men aren't going to get it right. I always watch the screen really closely when a story comes on about teachers or parents, and it's almost always women. They have actresses playing the part of construction workers and fighter

pilots so that girls will have role models; why not men as teachers and single parents? I'm a single dad.

Closely linked to the notion of changing the image of teaching from a "women only" occupation is the idea that more effort must go into reaching out to young males to demonstrate to them that men do, in fact, teach small children.

> Roger: You know, they don't point out what a wonderful life ... I'm mean, I'm honored. I truly am after all these years. I'll never burn out as a teacher because it's a great honor for me to work with kids every day. And I know there's nobody in the world more important than a teacher. But, I don't know if high school students, especially men, or young boys, or young teens, whatever you want to call 'em, I don't think they understand the value of the teaching profession, the joys of the teaching profession until they tried it.

Fred, a fifty-year-old, third-grade teacher, feels that the answer lies in the way we assign child-rearing tasks. Fred focuses on the institutionalized practices of teacher education.

> If I were king, I would wipe out every school of education and every university and start over because I think it starts there. When someone enters a school of education and they start looking at their career choices, I think they're guided, men, I think the bias starts there, guiding these guys deliberately away. Because I've talked to and had student teachers and they were given no encouragement when they went through the university system. They were given no opportunity or direc-

tion to say, "Hey, maybe that's an option." Change
entirely how, when they start education courses
and educational methodology at the university
level, to let these guys immerse themselves just as
much with an approach to elementary schools as
the high schools.

Javier agrees with Fred and gives a few more specific glimpses
into the student teachers' lives.

Javier: Even when I was going through teacher
training, I just got the feeling that everybody at the
school was just assuming that I would want to be
with the older children, high school or something
like that or ... even on little exercises and some of
the practical things we did in class, it was just real
easy for them to turn to the women, to talk to them
about children, and they engage in discussions with
female students. They just assume that they've had
lots of experience with small children and that ...
oh, I don't know, there was just a different way
when they would talk to me. There were a few men
that went through teacher training with me. I don't
know where they went.

Javier and Fred, like others who spoke with me, depict a
teacher-training environment in which it is assumed that the typical
student is female and, therefore, has likely had connections with
children and their needs. I have spoken with thirteen men currently
enrolled in teacher credential programs about their experiences thus
far. In general, their stories confirm what the teachers have been
telling me.[21]

The scarcity of men as instructors and mentors is not lost on the
students. They have nobody to guide them through the process of
becoming teachers.

Sam: Well, for one thing, I'm usually the only man. I get asked for the "male" point of view a lot. I get the sense that's a set up, so I just make a joke and avoid answering.

*****

Tim: I'd hoped to do my student teaching with a male, but that couldn't be arranged. To be honest, I'm not sure why. Two of the women were placed in men's classes. I haven't had the chance to be taught by a man even once.

Early in their training, men begin to receive unsolicited advice regarding their appropriateness for the upper grades, specialist positions, and, in particular, administration. There is considerable ambivalence on the men's part in deciding whether to take the remarks as kindly or as admonition. One thing they are confident about is that women do not receive these messages.

Rod: I think every teacher I've had has told me how to continue on to get my administrative credentials. I can't figure out what they're trying to tell me.

*****

Josh: I stopped telling them I plan to teach kindergarten. I either get "Oh, that's so sweet," or questions about how I'm going to handle being around the little kids—like I'm liable to go crazy because men can't stand kids.

The men are informed early on that their actions around children will be closely monitored and that this may not seem fair, but it is to be expected. The only form of abuse that the men say is emphasized is sexual molestation.

> You know, the topic of school safety comes up a
> lot. As soon as the talk drifts around to protecting
> the kids, I know the subject of molestation is com-
> ing. There is no question but that men are the tar-
> get, and I just feel like every eye is on me. We
> never discuss kids being slapped or pushed or
> called names. I don't dare to mention that in class.
> I brought it up in conversation and got attacked for
> supposedly trying to avoid the "real" issue.

John, like Keith above, goes further back into the way we
socialize girls and boys in elementary and secondary school.

> I think I would try to get guys in to experience the
> classroom. Even before that, let them, as kids, play
> parent. Like in my classroom, everyone gets en-
> couraged to take care of little children and to take
> care of the home. It's real hard to find picture
> books that even show males taking care of the fam-
> ily, you know? Except as the breadwinner.

Are we continuing to live a self-fulfilling prophecy about
women's work and men's work?[22] Are we, for example, hiring men
as teachers based on a gendered preconception of what they should
bring to the occupation and then structuring their work lives to
ensure that they not deviate from our plan for them? Some of the
most interesting applications of gender studies are those that pro-
pose how problematic maleness and masculinity are in a highly gendered social and intellectual context. It is possible that those who
choose to defy the usual world of gendered occupations have considered the ramifications and risks and are willing to share their
experiences with others if we are willing to set aside preconceptions
and listen with fresh ears. The interviews with men teachers suggest
that many men may place teaching and other forms of women's
work high on their list of desirable jobs and would pursue these
interests if free to do so.

Affirmative action for men makes little sense if we confine ourselves to a narrow definition of "quotas." Opponents of affirmative action for women and men of color often frame the argument in these limited terms to invoke the ire of the majority. Another criticism of affirmative action is that it is the members of the target group themselves who are choosing not to enter the field. If so, expending energies and resources to increase their participation would seem fruitless.

However, the resounding message that comes from the interviews is that action to remedy men's scarcity should consist of the broader, richer components of affirmative action: outreach, presentation of counter-stereotypical modeling, and activities to compensate for a lifetime devoid of contact with children. Child care in general, and early childhood education in particular, are not presented to boys and young men as being appropriate life endeavors. Simultaneously, boys and men are taught to eschew the kinds of personal rewards that can come from teaching and child care.

To summarize, I have presented some of the ways that the teachers tell me their work life is gendered. Some tasks are assigned, formally or informally, to men and others to women. While there was some division of labor for substantive teaching tasks—for example, being the "math guy"—most of the activities that the men described were non-teaching duties. Physical tasks, such as lifting and moving, are also seen as the men's responsibility. One of the most important tasks is the handling of disciplinary duties. The men all report that it is common practice to place children with behavioral problems in their classroom. Closely associated with this is the understanding that the men are expected to interact with authoritarian principals. Principalship itself has been constructed as an appropriate, and often expected, objective for the men.

The men's own perceptions of themselves indicate that they frequently feel they have talents in areas such as reading and art but must work to have these talents acknowledged. All but a few stated openly to me that disciplinary problems and adversarial roles with administrators are not compatible with their own definitions of self. They also reveal that "emotional support" duties are exclusively within the purview of the women.

The men's narratives contradict existing literature that says that men, upon entering the occupation, access a male network and step on a fast track to promotions. For one thing, the men deny having a strong desire to be promoted. In fact, the men spend considerable energy fending off suggestions that they are more appropriate for administrative positions. Second, the majority of the men's peers *and supervisors* are women, casting doubt on the existence of a readily available male network.

Finally, in their descriptions of hypothetical plans to increase the numbers of men in early teaching, the men reveal that there are deterrents to men entering teaching that are more instrumental than low pay: (1) at an early age, boys are directed away from activities that would hone child care skills, (2) teaching is a profession that is marketed to women more than men, (3) the image of teacher most prevalent in society is that of "mother" figure, making teaching an occupation for women, and (4) men feel that teacher education is geared toward women and women's supposed histories of having connections to children, causing many men to feel like interlopers.

Adding to the contradictory nature of these expectations is the idea that any attempt on the part of the men to deflect or resist stereotypically male activities results in increased doubts on the part of significant others. In the next chapter, many of these themes are revisited as I discuss the men's ambiguous relationship with being "male role models."

~ 5 ~

Male Role Models

When I started out in teaching, I prided myself on the fact that I was going to be a role model for kids. Now it's my greatest nightmare. It's an albatross around my neck.

—Sid, first-grade teacher

In the last chapter I outlined some of the areas that presented conflict for the men teachers. Their lack of interest in being promoted, which might have confirmed their commitment to the children (real teachers), is often taken as an indication of their lack of appropriate drive and initiative (not real men). Any reluctance to perform physical tasks or to accept unruly kids can cause tension between them and their women peers. Their acceptance of these practices reproduces the conditions that support the stereotypes.

The focus of this chapter is the men's negotiation of the issue of modeling behavior, of being "role models." In my interactions with the teachers, the topic of "male role model" arose in every interview. When I examined my transcripts of individual interviews, I found that it was the teachers themselves, never I, who brought the term into the conversation. In the focus groups, I had presented the teachers with a draft of the emerging themes, and "role model" was listed there. I had anticipated the topic of role model from reading the literature but was surprised at the actual complexity of the concept as it is used by the men. There is not a single image of the male role model but several, and these are often ambiguous and contradictory.

The men see themselves as being expected to act as surrogate fathers for many of the children. The model they say they present to boys is different, however, from the one they display for girls in their classroom. There is also a difference between these models and the models they say they provide in response to parents' expectations. In addition, the men also describe obligations that they feel are associated with being the first male teacher for the children. Finally, many define themselves in terms of being a "token male," the model they present to their peers.

Modeling for Boys

The most striking feature of the men's descriptions of modeling for boys is lack of detail. As I show below, the men used very specific language to detail the behaviors and attitudes that they perceived were necessary to meet the girls' needs and to respond to the needs of parents, particularly single mothers raising sons. The descriptions of the modeling needs of boys, however, are colorless and vague and lack any sense of being proactive. They often say, like Manuel does, that as long as the person in the classroom is biologically male, the boys will be getting what they need.

> Manuel: But there's no way of stepping out of being a male role model because you are a male. You're always going to be referred to as a male role model in education, I think.
>
> Paul: No matter what you do?
>
> Manuel: Right, no matter what you do, you're a male role model.

More typically, the men described the concept in terms of "what everyone knows" to be true about males and male modeling.[1]

> Jake: I think it's good to have their child in front of a male watching them function. This is what adult men do. You're in their class for six hours a day, and I think it's advantageous for kids that don't have a male around their house. That's a role model.

Statements such as this include little explanation or description. They simply say that being an adult male in contact with boys is what is needed and asked for. As with Manuel, the men are explicitly saying that their physical presence repairs the absence of men at home. Exactly how this supposedly works is not clear to me, or, apparently, to the men. But it is clear that they are telling me that they believe that they are fulfilling others' expectations in this area simply by being a biologically male presence. Interestingly, none of the men noted that most of the boys' teachers were women, causing the men also to fill a void at school.

Modeling for Girls

For the girls in their classrooms, the men were far more explicit about their presentation of self. Early in the project I noticed that, in answer to my questions regarding interaction with the children, the men focused on their responsibilities toward "fatherless boys." Once I felt a man had told his story about this aspect of his life, I asked specifically about his responsibility to model for girls in the class-room. In most cases, the men could articulate fairly detailed descriptions of the type of masculinity they wanted to present or counter and, often, the game plan they carried out to accomplish it. The image they said they were fighting against is an ugly one. It depicts men as abusers and abandoners. Frank (second-grade teacher) told me:

I hope I rub off on the boys, and I hope I leave the girls with a positive image of men.

Paul: Can you describe the image you think they have of men?

Frank: Well, this is going to sound sexist, but I think a lot of the kids hear some pretty shitty things about men around their homes. And I'm not just talking about single-mother households, either. A lot of these kids live in homes where dad is gone all day and a large part of the evening, and mom just bitches about him constantly. I hear things from some of these kids that they could not possibly have thought up themselves—about dad not doing anything around the house, never home, can't be counted on. The first time I heard some of this, I just assumed that these were kids of a divorce. But no, dad and mom are both there.

Most often, the men felt that they were actually responding to the needs of the girls as presented by the parents, usually mothers. The mothers were likely to suggest what they felt the child needed, and the teachers said they tried to comply. Again, the girls' needs were specified only to the extent that there was to be a man in the girl's life and that the man was not to behave in rough or abusive ways.

This point was illustrated by Dave, a third-grade teacher, and Keith, who teaches first grade.

Dave: They need to see that men are not the kind of people that will leave their families, um, that will beat their kids, that will withhold their child support, that will get drunk on Friday nights, or whatever.

*****

Keith: And all I'm providing is an alternate. Or supplemental male role model so that they can grow up having experience with other males. (Using a child's voice): "Oh, well, I know my daddy, and now I know my teacher, and they're both males. And they're alike in some ways, and they're very different in some ways."

Typically, answers regarding interactions with girls were framed in a more proactive form of speech than responses about boys. More of the teachers expressed the idea that they consciously constructed their presentation of self to girls and that this construction involved an element of counter-stereotyping. There is considerable conflict between modeling stereotypical and counter-stereotypical behaviors, especially with both boys and girls in the same classroom.

Modeling for Parents

The proportion of children who are growing up in single-parent households is on the increase. Most of these single parents are women, and almost every teacher I interviewed told me that these parents expressed relief that their sons would have a male influence. Sometimes the expectations of the parent ran counter to the kind of person the teacher perceived himself to be. Javier, a third-grade teacher, echoed what became a common theme in these interviews.

I've had so many parents, especially single moms, come in and tell me how happy they are that their son is going to have a male teacher. I asked one woman why that made her so happy, and she told me she was becoming concerned because her son was getting into art and poetry a little too much. God, I love poetry and try to get all my students hooked on it. I didn't know what to say to her.

Nor was the ambiguity of the situation lost on Keith, a gay man who teaches first grade.

> You know, it begs the question, like, well, what is their standard? 'Cause it's all, you know, in the eye of the beholder. What is their standard of masculinity? What is masculine to them? If it's the testosterone, beer-drinking, football-playing, bowling-night-on-Wednesday, and poker-night-on-Friday, you know, smoking-the-cigars men, that ain't me, you know. [Laughs.]

Modeling masculinity is tricky. Most of the parents seem to be saying that their sons are not being exposed to real men behaving in real male ways outside of school. There is no actual attempt to explain what, exactly, they want their sons to experience. Instead, the implicit problem appears to be that the boys are seeing only women living out their lives on a day-to-day basis.

Nancy Chodorow and other object relations theorists would support this assessment saying that, since boys are reared primarily by women, they must learn their masculinity from some abstract concept, either through popular media or from their peers, with a resultant "blind leading the blind" scenario.[2] In addition, boys learn to be masculine by avoiding anything feminine.[3] This was very clear in my research. Both the teachers and the male students come under suspicion if they demonstrate feminine behaviors or interests.

In my interviews, several themes emerged that, together, form a model the parents are hoping the men teachers will bring to the classroom. Here is a list of desired attributes for men who teach boys:

1. Show no interest in art and poetry.
2. Be "the man in their lives."
3. Have interest in athletics.
4. Be a disciplinarian.
5. Be an authority figure.

In sum, the men are saying that, according to their understanding of the parents, what is missing in the boys' lives, and what the men are to provide, is someone who displays stereotypically male behaviors and attributes.

Occasionally a mother will tell a teacher that there is an undesirable adult male in the boy's life. In rare cases, the man may be into illegal or dangerous activities, but more typically he is deemed "irresponsible," that is to say, unemployed. None of the teachers spoke of parents who expressed a desire for a "new" man (e.g., artistic, nurturing, or emotionally expressive) to enter the boys' lives.

It was not just children of single parents who would supposedly benefit from a male role model. Roger, a kindergarten teacher, can compare his time teaching in an impoverished area with his current assignment in a school predominately populated by children from upper socioeconomic strata.

> What we find in this area ... and this is my personal insight, we find in this area that's very affluent that the majority of mothers stay in the home, choose to work at home, or work as a housewife, if you will, and so the fathers are out there being doctors and lawyers and they work A LOT! It's my opinion that these students don't have a lot of interaction with their fathers, and so I kind of take that on. I don't, no, I don't take that on, I fill that role for them, I think, in many capacities.

Even in the case of the father who is absent because of work responsibilities, the teachers feel they are expected to model the kind of masculinity these fathers would likely portray if they were more available. This is paradoxical since it is the workaholic father's adherence to dominant models of masculine success that is at the root of his emphasis of work over family. Perhaps the mothers feel that their sons will have a real, prescriptive model present in their lives to augment the abstract model created by their fathers' absence.

Adding to the confusion is that most of the men teachers

describe themselves using "feminine" attributes and descriptors. When I asked about the contradictory nature of their position *vis-à-vis* these descriptions, they were at a loss to explain it. These men simply live through the contradictions.

> Bill: I think I exhibit more female qualities because I cross that stereotypical male line.

*****

> Don: It's not that I set aside to preach certain values in my classroom, I don't do that, but it's the daily, "Be nice to your classmates, be nice to your friends, cooperation, caring, kindness." These things are pretty important to society.

The dialogue between Manuel and me is typical of what transpired whenever I tried to clear the air on the contradictory nature of their descriptions of role models. Manuel had just told me that there were people who felt that children need a male role model in order to experience being in the presence of someone who demonstrates "maleness."

> Manuel: I'm portraying myself the way I feel every person should, male or female. Caring human being taking care of children, showing how to be kind and value one another, cooperate.

> Paul: It sounds like your definition of male role model is different from that of the people who are actively trying to put kids in your classroom.

> Manuel: Clarify their definition.

> Paul: Well, that's what I'm after. I'm trying to figure out what it is that is included in the male role model that would induce somebody to think it

would be beneficial to specifically put a kid in your class. The things you're telling me, a female would stereotypically be more likely to provide.

Manuel: I don't know. I think, again, this is something that I didn't ask for. I didn't ask for that. I almost feel like Charles Barkley when he says, "Hey, we didn't ask to be role models," but it's part of my job. I do understand that. I see my role as perhaps being, for a lot of ... for all my students, maybe the father figure they don't have. And that's an interesting thing to say. That's an ironic thing for me to say considering I don't have children of my own, and especially when I have parents who come and ask for advice on parenting.

Whenever I would ask for clarification on the concept of male role model, the men would typically ask me to define what I meant by the term. I had to remind them that it was they, not I, who had originally brought the term into the conversation and that they already explained to me that they were trying to comply with the needs of parents or others. The concept is so uncritically embedded in their discourse that they do not feel it needs any explanation. It appears to be standard teacher jargon and is used as a term that covers a host of unspecified attributes and behaviors associated with men as teachers.

In listening to the men it became clear that the puzzle of the origins of gender relations was not new to them. While they did not describe gender in terms of its salience, or centrality, in organizing and constructing particular moments of their lives, it was evident that they have given some thought to theories about gender.[4] Their underlying assumptions about gender were revealed during their discussions of the male role model issue. As I considered their various positions on gender relations, it occurred to me that they were likely exposed to the variety of gender theories that have now been labeled "sex-role theory." While role theory, particularly as it is applied to gender, has been criticized for its rigidity and avoidance of power issues, its explanatory power when integrated into local "folk theories" cannot be dismissed.[5] For those of us who engage in ethnographic research, it is imperative that we attempt to see the world as our informants see it, and that includes being sensitive to the perspectives they have adopted to help them explain their world and their positions in it.

The place of male role model in the lives of these men cannot be fully understood without examining how sex-role theory informs their views of teaching and gender. Sex-role theory says men and women must acquire certain attributes appropriate for their sex in order to be validated as members of their sex.[6] The basic process of acquiring one's role is described in terms of "agents" (e.g., the family, schools, peer groups, and mass media) that act as sources for integrating the requisite beliefs, skills, and values into the consciousness.[7]

> Norman: There's no male role model, no father figure, and so they think that, by having a child in a class with a male teacher, their child will get some male-ness rubbed off on them.

Supposedly feminine and masculine roles are learned and internalized. Tim Carrigan, Robert Connell, and John Lee criticize this idea because so few women and men actually live up to the roles. They see role theory as descriptive of differences in the abstract (e.g., stereotypes) rather than of actual relations between women and men.[8]

Interestingly, in describing the history and application of sex-role theory, Joseph Pleck calls on the history of teaching and especially the ideas of Horace Mann, who suggested that the increase in the number of women elementary school teachers, part of the general changing roles of women in the late nineteenth century, was at the heart of the fear of boys and men becoming "feminized."[9] Eduardo's experiences have provided him with evidence that makes him suspicious of this idea.

> I hear that term [male role model] a lot. I'm not
> exactly sure. I mean I'm conscious of my male-
> ness. I come in and I teach, and I realize there is
> some talk that it is good for some of the boys to
> have men in the classroom because they're basi-
> cally surrounded by women otherwise. I've never
> really thought about it much. I know that some of
> the studies I've read have said that it doesn't really
> make any difference, that boys do just as well with
> male teachers as female teachers.

Sex-role theory has been basically ahistorical, devoid of com-
parisons of cross-cultural gender constructions and uncritical of the
way male-female interactions construct masculinities and femininities.[10] In fact, sex-role theory does not allow for an analysis of multiple masculinities and femininities, settling instead for a definition
of two monolithic categories that rest on a superficial analysis of
human personality and motives.[11]

> Adam: They [single mothers] are, for the most part,
> happy that there's a role model because they feel
> that they can't model a male behavior for them.
> And they feel they want the child to model adult
> male behavior.

Talcott Parsons and Robert Bales' ideas of "expressive" and
"instrumental" roles lie at the foundation of much of the sex-role
paradigm. Their functionalist, and highly conservative, model has
contributed to the idea that women and men lead opposite and com-
plementary lives—what Sherry Ortner calls "separate spheres."[12]
This polarity is especially evident in the privileged position granted
heterosexual relations in Parsons and Bales' work.[13]

Proponents of role theory point to evidence of differential treatment of children, based on sex, as a primary influence in the development of different interests, skills, and personalities in males and
females. Same-sex modeling is an important issue since evidence

shows that most children are raised primarily by women, leaving boys to model after some abstract notion of masculinity. In effect, boys are modeling themselves after masculine stereotypes rather than after real men.[14]

Understanding these theories helps us to understand how the men teachers negotiate what they perceive to be gender issues in their daily work lives because the teachers evidently used these theories, in various combinations, in responding to my queries regarding the gendered nature of their work lives. It is not possible to determine how much of an active part these same perspectives played in their daily lives, but several points are clear. First, the men refer to the roles for men and women in terms of expectations, prescriptions, and proscriptions, rather than in terms of some innate difference between women and men. Second, they see the roles as something that has been assigned them, rather than something that they themselves have constructed independent of the structure of teaching. Third, the use of the role jargon appears to allow the men to communicate imprecise thoughts and feelings in generic symbolic terms, superficially accepted by most, critically understood by few. Last, the idea that roles emanate from some source outside the men, despite the vagueness of the actual source, helps the men to question the source, rather than themselves, when they feel they are not conforming perfectly to guidelines. The consequence appears to be a kind of passive resistance on the part of the men, rather than any overt attack on the system. This "quiet movement" of men questioning gender roles for men needs our attention, and I will return to it in greater detail in the last chapter.[15]

First Male, Only Male, and Token Male

Aside from the role modeling issues presented above, the men were likely to describe their experiences as the children's "first male teacher," the school's "only male teacher," or the "token male." While a more complete assessment of the cultural context associated with these terms is presented in Chapter Six, some aspects of these descriptions are pertinent to the discussion of role models presented here. As I pointed out in the previous section, "role" seems to be an easy communication vehicle for the men to use in the absence of an appropriate vocabulary for their changing lives.

First Male. The men see themselves as "the first male teacher" to whom the kids have been exposed. Chuck, a first-grade teacher, was telling me about parents' reactions to finding out their children will have a man teacher.

> The only thing I've heard is some'll say, "He's looking forward to having you," or "He (or she) really enjoys being in your class because you're the first male teacher they've had." That's the only thing I've ever heard.

The first time I heard this from a teacher was during an interview with a fifth-grade teacher from my previous research in elementary schools. This seemed so commonsensical to me that I simply logged it and moved on. "Of course," I thought to myself, "with only a tenth of the teachers being men, the chances are very good that a child will not encounter a man until later grades." This is a fine example of what can happen to researchers when we do not remain what I have come to call "freshly critical" throughout our analysis. By this I mean that we must endeavor to approach each bit of data anew every time we encounter it, no matter how many times we encounter it.

When teachers in this current study made reference to being a child's first male teacher, I again let it pass until Chuck said it. I still might not have seen any significance had Chuck not been talking about the responsibility of early educators as socializers. He was explaining that the primary grades set the pace for the children's educational experience. He remarked that as a first-grade teacher, he was the first full-day teacher for the kids and, thus, felt obligated to instill the kinds of habits and attitudes that will help the kids succeed in school. During transcription, the two statements regarding "first" were in close enough physical proximity on the page that they caught my eye.

Even if teaching were composed equally of men and women, it would be perfectly reasonable to expect that many children would not encounter a man until first grade. There is nothing remarkable about being the *second* teacher. One of the kindergarten teachers, Norman, made this statement.

> Since I'm often the kid's first male teacher, I can understand that there might be some questions in the parents' minds.

Of the nine teachers who told me they were the first male teacher, three teach third grade, one teaches second, four first, and one kindergarten. What is interesting about "first" statements coming from Chuck and other early grade teachers is that the identification with the status of first male teacher appears to be more than just a statement of demographics. The men appear to see this as a responsibility to the students, the parents, and the school. They are saying that they see "first" as an obligation to perform in certain ways. This links directly with the theme of male role model. The men generally see themselves as representative of what men could (should) offer children. It is likely that the men perceive that they are the first male primary teacher encountered by the *parents* of the children. This became clearer when I questioned the remainder of the men who made the statement. For example, John told me, "Well, I guess I feel that the parents have other children in the system and so know there aren't other males at the school." John is telling us that his assessment of his responsibilities toward the kids is based on a socially constructed identity, one that he perceives must exist.

Only Male. Many of the men also describe themselves as the "only male" on site or at least at their grade level. Almost all of them mentioned several school sites at which no men taught at any primary levels and a few others where there were no men teachers at all. A quick scan of the directory out of which I worked showed that, indeed, of the 146 schools from which I drew my informants, almost 100 had no men teaching at the primary level and 30 had no men teachers at any level. In addition to the men's perceptions of gender demographics, which are often correct, the scarcity of men sets the stage for what the men perceive as another level of modeling for which they feel responsible. These teachers feel that they are expected to perform certain teaching and support tasks *because they are the only men*. They listed such duties as handling discipline problems, performing much of the manual labor and stereotypical male tasks, and acting as liaison with men principals. Their presentation of these tasks was often prefaced by a phrase such as "Being the only male...." As Norman (a kindergarten teacher) told me,

> I understand them [young single mothers]. I'm the only male here. In their shoes, I think what they're saying is, "You know, life's hard. I'm trying to raise this boy by myself. I live in an area where there are gangs all over the place, people get shot every now and then, and, you know, my boy is even talking back to me already. I need a man." This is how I think the parent would think.

Token Male. Over half the teachers referred to themselves as a "token male" in their stories. While sometimes their form of reference appeared to be almost farcical, they also presented what they felt were some very serious consequences of being the only man.

> Fred: Well, I'm kinda the token male on campus. I take a lot of stuff about that ... about being a representative of all the men the teachers have ever known [laughs]. Like just today, at a meeting, one of the women said, "Hey, Fred, we need the male perspective here." Sometimes they just blow me off the same way. "Oh, Fred, that's just the male view."

*****

> Allen: I do feel like, um.... I do feel like a lot of the female teachers [voice lowers], um.... Recently we

had a reorganization where I became a one/two and
a teacher sent quite a few males to me in this reorganization, and I was concerned about the gender
composition of the class and she mentioned that
she felt that these students would be better off with
me, the only male role model which, I don't know,
I kind of looked at it and said, "Well, wait a minute
we both do the same things, we're paid to do the
same things. [Laughs.] Why is this the situation
that exists?"

Rosabeth Moss Kanter describes the phenomenon of
"tokenism" for women in predominantly male occupations in terms
of the effects of being in the minority. Several things occur under
these conditions of "underrepresentedness." First, the majority
group is likely to view the minority group in terms of their "master
status," as defined by the majority. Gender is the salient status for
the men in my study, just as it was for the women in Industrial
Supply Corporation, the focus of Kanter's research. The minority
members find themselves put on display, asked to speak for and
answer for their entire group, and are expected to play out the stereotypical performances seen as integral to their group. In addition, the
minority members are not seen to be as trustworthy as the majority.
Kanter borrows Wilbert Moore's concept of "homosocial reproduction" to call attention to the use of "sameness" as a criterion for
trustworthiness. Over time, the leaders of an organization become a
homogeneous core who increasingly distrust "outsiders."[16] An
important component of tokenism is that the minority members are
often singled out, stigmatized even, for the "offense" of behaving in
the same manner as the majority. This "double bind" acts to accen-
tuate the differences between the majority and minority and brings
focus back onto the perceived differences.
    Men teachers present some "problems" to the teaching realm
that are part of a "composite portrait" of a minority group, who are
always seen and treated as a homogeneous category, profoundly different from the majority.[17] Kanter refers to the dominant's (major-

ity's) tendency to "heighten the boundaries" between them and the minority group by emphasizing their own commonalties while stressing the minority's difference.[18]

In researching men nurses, Christine Williams says she found that it was the "*men* who attempt to construct boundaries separating themselves from their female majority."[19] In general, she says, men have a positive experience and are treated well by the female majority. However, she goes on to present several pieces of evidence that are supportive of the strict interpretation of Kanter's model showing that it is indeed the majority group that heightens boundaries. For example, men nurses were assigned more heavy lifting, were expected to specialize in care of male patients rather than a more generalist set of assignments, and were left out of the social activities. As with the men teachers I interviewed, men nurses received unsolicited advice and encouragement to pursue more administrative or technical positions rather than intimate bedside care. Williams says: "With few notable exceptions, nursing educators are enthusiastic and supportive of their male students." Yet she includes the following quote from a "thirty-eight-year-old nurse."

> I was encouraged from square one. The lady who was the director of the nursing program ... was encouraging, as were most of the educators, to any man who was seriously interested in becoming a RN. In fact, she was pushing us both [himself and the other male student in his class] to go on and get our master's and teach, do legislative work, or some other pertinent nurse-advocate work.[20]

The teachers do not perceive their supposed suitability for administrative positions as an advantage. When we take into account the men's explicit denial of any desire to be promoted, their rejection of the stereotypical attributes associated with administrators, and the powerful proscriptions against touching and generally nurturing the children, the real message that emerges is that men are seen as less than suitable for the day-to-day care of and contact with children. This point is made more clear in the ways that homophobia and fears of pedophilia actively affect the men's lives. As was pointed out by some of the teachers in my study and, in Williams' work, some nurses, the message concerning appropriateness for other positions begins early in training, as a kind of tracking.

In Kanter's model of tokenism, the consequence of women's minority status linked with the overall masculine culture is that women are ultimately denied the positions to which they have every right to aspire.[21] In the case of the men teachers, it is easy to overlook that they, too, are often being denied the position most important to them—being a real teacher, as Jake desires to be.

> It's real common for somebody to come get me because they want the male side of an issue. Sometimes that bothers me. I'd prefer to be seen as a teacher, a GOOD teacher, mostly.

Embedded in the notion that men should value promotions is the idea that teaching (and women's work in general) is of lower value than men's work and therefore is inappropriate for a society's breadwinners. But individual social actors, women and men, cannot be held accountable for an existing societal division of labor that puts more material value on administration than on teaching. This is victim-blaming. In this case, the blaming may take the form of dismissing any harm to which the men may lay claim since they appear to benefit ultimately by acquiring positions that are often closed to women.[22] The men in my study indicate that the price for attaining more valued positions may be too great for some men to pay. In the specific case of men in elementary school teaching, the price they would have to pay for promotions is to give up their lives with the children. Unfortunately, the price the men are paying for remaining in teaching is to live under a constant cloud of suspicion. Could this price be too high for many men, and is this price the reason many are turning away?[23]

In summary, Jim Allan found that men teachers are faced with conflict and contradictions in trying to walk a very thin line between hyper- and hypo-masculinity. Allan's fear is that men are being forced out of elementary teaching by strong gender presence. The men's leaving reproduces the gendered structure of the occupation.[24] Kelvin Seifert discusses the contradiction involved in hiring more men to provide role models. If nurturing men are hired, they will not reflect the model that many parents are asking for—a traditional male.[25]

Christine Williams discovered that when workers enter gender-atypical occupations, they do not change the gendered nature of the occupation at all but somehow manage to re-negotiate the internal workings so that they actually emphasize their own stereotypical gendered characteristics.[26] For teachers, often this involves treading a delicately fine path between displaying enough maleness to satisfy the perceived needs of children from fatherless homes (and to allay any suspicions) and providing the kind of warmth and closeness to meet the needs of young children.

We need to look at how men negotiate these contradictions between being "real men" and "real teachers." Dolores Gold and Myrna Reis surveyed the empirical research on two issues: the effects of gender on children and the relative masculinity of men in a predominately female occupation. They found no significant advantage in having men teach. Their conclusion, however, is based on the finding that boys with men teachers didn't score any higher on tests for masculine sex-role identification than boys with women teachers.[27] The literature on which Gold and Reis focused involved the psychological testing, in use since the 1930s, designed to evaluate the impact of the "feminization" of the world of boys and the possible resultant hypo- or hyper-masculinity.[28] Gold and Reis took the position that there is no advantage to hiring men teachers. On the other hand, their own meta-analysis could be interpreted to demonstrate that men do not seem to pass on stereotypical behaviors any more than women do. Therefore, there is certainly no *disadvantage* to hiring men, either.

Much of the literature seems to have legitimized some "folk theories" regarding men teachers. One is that some men are just "doing time" until they can get promoted to more lucrative, powerful positions. Another is that those who are interested in doing women's work are effeminate. Unfortunately, these theories ignore the real lived experiences of men who teach.[29] We need inquiries into the consequences arising from these myths. The men themselves must negotiate around, through, and in response to these myths, resulting in excessive effort to do gender while doing their jobs.

Hiring men as role models seems, on the surface, an admirable mission and has been the topic of numerous newspaper articles and columns. There is, however, no unified definition of male role model and no single way for a man to live up the responsibilities implied by the term. Instead, the concept is actually a convenient label for a collection of contradictions that are embedded in the lives of men caught between portraying stereotypical and counter-stereotypical masculine behaviors and between being real men and real teachers.

~ 6 ~

The Culture of Primary Teaching

I know something about Rosa Parks now, something I never knew before: I know how she felt, that hot day in the back of the bus.
—Paul, elementary education major[1]

The stories told thus far contradict the usual accounts that explain men's underrepresentation in primary education. Working under intense scrutiny, being assigned gender-specific tasks, and responding to ambiguous requirements to act as role models combine to create an occupational environment that does not facilitate the easy entry and retention of men. The men I interviewed are reluctant to discuss their problems and fears with anybody, including their peers. Their general isolation also seems to contribute to a lack of vocabulary with which to discuss their situation. The cumulative effects of the themes that have emerged contribute to their lack of fit in the culture of primary teaching. These findings, and their cumulative effects, have important implications for increasing the participation of men in early education.

Silence

Very few teachers openly discuss the issues told to me in the individual interviews. Javier's response to my query about speaking to others regarding the issues that he presented in the interview is the most complete statement of any by a single participant. I purposely left in all of Javier's stumblings, hesitations, and obvious difficulties in finding the right words to demonstrate how these otherwise eloquent men become poor communicators over the subject of their ambivalence regarding differential treatment. His lengthy statement on the matter is unique in that it encompasses several of the themes that arose across the interviews. They appear in the following order in Javier's statement: (1) silence, (2) scrutiny, (3) division of labor, (4) scarcity of men, (5) lack of fit, (6) isolation, and (7) scrutiny (again).

> Javier: Um, I really couldn't ... I really can't talk about some of this stuff to, uh, female peers. You know, some of this stuff just comes out wrong and, uh ... you know ... very ... they don't really ... I'm sure they don't see it as a big issue that, uh ... you know, I feel more watched, or more closely monitored than they do around the children. It's just sort of what we accept as the rule. I, um ... I, uh ... I certainly can't ... I'm not ... I wouldn't complain to them about carrying things, moving stuff, I mean, uh ... you know, it's kind of hard enough as it is, uh....

> Paul: What's hard enough?

> Javier: Well, you know, with all of the, oh ... you know, the, uh, sex ... harassment things going on out there and, you know, there are some pretty creepy things happening to women in workplaces and stuff and, uh ... and, uh ... you know, here at this workplace women are in the majority but, uh

… uh … you know, they still feel as though they're not getting a … you know, an even break out there in the world in general quite often, and sometimes I get the brunt of that. Uh … you know, just little things. "Oh, it figures a man would say that." That kind of stuff. Um, I don't … I try not to let it, uh, let it bother me. Well, yeah, it really does bother me sometimes. Um, yeah, I think it would be interesting to talk with some other male teachers. Gosh, I don't know why, uh, why I haven't done that except that it just seems like it would be, I don't know, could be construed as being rabble rousing or something.

The men often disclosed that any questioning on their part will contribute to the already high level of scrutiny under which they work.

Frank: I feel I'm less capable of understanding the girls because I've got limited contact with them. I don't think I've ever expressed that before.

Paul: Why is that?

Frank: Well, think about how it sounds, a male complaining about not getting enough time with the little girls. There's no one to complain to.

*****

Eduardo: I haven't told this to anyone but my wife. I don't dare to complain to anyone about the issue. I mean, the only ones I think would support me are those who are technically breaking the rules by doing too much touching. I don't want to cause them trouble. I just want to be able to teach the same way they do. But I can't go in and demand the right to touch kids more.

From the men's perspective, the division of tasks and the differential enforcement of "touching" rules are problems, but calling attention to the problems will only increase the likelihood that the men will be suspected of being unfit to teach.

The men often feel that they are dealing with issues that are so embedded in the taken-for-granted culture of teaching that the points are considered self-explanatory and, through the act of questioning, they are demonstrating either complete ignorance of the basic concepts of teaching or perhaps showing a desire to run counter to the accepted practices. Either of these would, again, contribute to the general suspicion regarding the appropriateness of the man for teaching.

> Eduardo: I even got lectured to by one of the district staff. I was told outright that, as a man, my actions with children are, of course, more open to criticism. Why "of course"?

> *****

> George: There's really no discussing this with anyone. They respond with an attitude of "you really should know this by now," and that kinda cuts off any further conversation or negotiation. That's just the way it is.

> *****

> Adam: They don't give any explanation, just give me that "of course this should make perfect sense" look.

Eduardo's question, "Why of 'course'?" points to a deeper dissatisfaction than simply that attached to being under scrutiny. It also indicates that the men are unhappy with principles so embedded in the teaching culture that they apparently need no further explanation, even on that rare occasion when someone protests. Because they are so uncritically entrenched and the men are unlikely to take the considerable risks associated with raising such issues, there appears to be little hope that these issues will get a public hearing in the foreseeable future.

The disparity in enforcement adds to the overall construction of separate spheres for men and women teachers.[2] When the men say there is "no one" to talk to about the matters they've expressed, they are indicating that the women with whom they work would not be capable of understanding the men's perspective since the women are not operating under the same cloud of suspicion.

In the focus groups, however, the men elaborated their concerns about being under scrutiny. For many of them, this was perhaps the first time that they had felt safe to voice these feelings openly without their words being taken the wrong way. The value and importance of the men having the opportunity to talk among themselves is discussed below, under "isolation."

> Javier: Actually I don't think I've ever talked to any other male teacher about teaching in particular, or at least nothing ... no specifics. I've certainly never talked to anybody about the things we've talked about here today.

*****

> Barry: I tell you, some of what's been said here could really be taken the wrong way. I'm nervous talking about it. But I'm a little angry that I can't talk about it.

The contrast between the above statements, made in the group setting, and those made to me in private is informative. Although the men were more likely to confide in me in personal interviews that they were frightened or hurt, their communication style was closed and secretive and there was not the air of "rebellion" that arose in the group interviews. As the group interaction became more focused, the approach changed from one of supposedly understanding the need for scrutiny to one of posing its unfairness. Both speech and behavior provided evidence that the men normally see their criticism of some of the teaching practices to be fraught with danger. The following come from individual interviews.

> Jake: That's a whole can of worms right there. There's things I just don't do.
>
> Paul: It must be a can of worms; you backed away from the microphone.
>
> Jake: Yeah, yeah [laugh], you could tell from my body language.

*****

> Roger: It [child's artwork] might be the ugliest thing in the world, but it's true art because every single child has a different sample. You know, I love that. But, uh, I'm not very cutesy [laughs], but I.... It's a sexist comment, but nobody'll know I said that, right?

I kept a field journal in which I recorded my early perceptions of each interview. In addition, when I listened to the taped interviews, I wrote down the images that came to mind of the men and their environment. In reviewing these notes, I find that over half the men, when discussing the more sensitive issues I've listed, displayed body language that indicated that they were apprehensive about discussing them. I found such entries as "voice lowers," "looks about for possible witnesses," and "looks at microphone."

Reluctance is not the only reason the men do not discuss these sensitive topics. They apparently lack a vocabulary that would allow them to communicate some of their experiences to others. I was taken with their struggles to find the right words to express how they perceive their situations. Often, they tried to draw on the language of women in male-dominated occupations, which, they asserted, was not accurate, but would have to suffice. Anne Minas calls this "language drift." She contends that past experiences shape our beliefs which, in turn, affect how we experience new things. The problem with using old language to describe new phenomena is that we are likely to attach the old meanings to new situations through the use of outdated terms. The significance of the change that has taken place is often lost in this way. Minas says we need to concern ourselves with the institutions to which we belong, often by choice, and which affect our choices and us. Her definition of "basic" is anything that is experiential and understood without special knowledge.[3] The language (meaning) of gender can be modified as a consequence of social change. But though situations change, we don't necessarily develop a new vocabulary to describe them. Instead, we try to modify existing terms.

> Nate: I'm sure some people would laugh at the idea, but I feel as though I'm being discriminated against when it comes to interacting with the kids. I guess that might not be the best word, but it's the only one I can think of to describe what happens to me.

Nate's use of the word "discrimination" is illustrative of the feelings demonstrated by most of the men. If we apply the definition of discrimination that is in general use in the social sciences, we can indeed argue that men are discriminated against in early education. They face institutionalized barriers to success that are embedded in the occupation and create obstacles that other groups do not face. In spite of their statements attesting to their acceptance of closer scrutiny, the teachers harbor considerable resentment over it.

> Mike: Well, you know, I think that it's really what made me want to talk to you, not made me want to talk to you, but when I got your letter, just the whole idea of males in education and the things that go on, the reverse, um ... I want to call ... it's a reversal of roles. When it's a predominantly female situation ... that nowadays goes on in the

workplace that if it was male-oriented or male-dominated and it happened, that women would immediately go, "Sexual harassment!" Those things happen
in teaching, but because it's the males, we don't
jump up and go "Sexual harassment."

*****

Adam: I myself don't [talk with women teachers
about the situation]. And I really don't because,
usually female teachers ... anything that you say
that they're not really liking ... they have a little
sense of female support about how, you know, they
virtually can say or do anything, they can do any
sexual harassment, they can do it whenever they
want, they can say any sexually related thing any-
time they want. They can make any, I don't want to
say chauvinistic, but, you know, gender stereotypical comment any time they want freely, and of
course men do not have that same option back. In
fact, we don't have that option at all.

The idea that women teachers were thought to "harass" the men
teachers came as a complete surprise to me, and initially I kept listening for some indications that the men were joking. Instead, I
came to realize that they have real concerns about the way that some
of the women teachers speak to them, speak of them, and treat them.
This is a major theme of the "cultural fit" section below.

Isolation

Men teachers have few daily connections with other men in the
profession. While isolation in general is a concern for all teachers,
as my earliest surveys demonstrated, men teachers are especially
affected because of their fewness. This limited contact with others
who might share their experiences and concerns may be a partial

cause of their language deficit because it leaves men without the means to formulate ways to express themselves. In addition, each man is left to deal individually with the frustrations arising from the contradictions internal to the occupation. With each man working independently, no general plan for relief can be formulated.

> Keith: So there's four classroom teachers out of twelve or thirteen classrooms, so a third of the teachers are male.

> Paul: That's very high.

> Keith: It is high. I mean, especially since lately I was talking about transferring to another school. I said, "Well, you know, what's it like there?" and they said, "There are no men." NONE! NO MALE TEACHERS in that school, and there's like 23 teachers. So I thought, I don't know if I could do that.

> Paul: Why?

> Keith: I don't think I would want to be the ONLY male. I get along well with women, but, you know, it's kinda like ... I like the diversity. I don't want to be the token male.

In the school districts I targeted there were approximately one hundred sites at which there were no men teaching at the primary level. Thirty schools have no men teachers at any level.

> Norman: Sometimes I think I kind of miss that, that I don't have a group of guys that I can hang out with. But, you know basically I kind of just go out, do my thing at school, and then get myself back to the beach as fast as possible.

Like many men teachers in my study, Norman confines his school time to his obligatory classroom tasks. Dave specifically rules out socializing with other teachers.

> Dave: More and more, I've gotten away from
> doing the social aspect of interacting with my
> peers.... It's just not satisfying any more.

Leonard Chusmir, in interviews with men who have made non-traditional career choices, also found that men teachers tended to feel isolated.[4] Since there is almost no contact with other men, and relatively little interaction with women peers regarding the issues the men spoke about with me, it is not surprising that these issues have gotten scant attention in terms of making changes.

In an environment where one gender predominates, the diversity among the minority members may not be evident. This is one of the aspects of tokenism. Each man in the elementary school culture is perceived and treated in stereotypical ways. As a result, the men tend to act in more stereotypical fashion than they would if unconstrained. In particular, men are likely to refrain from showing deep-felt emotions since they are reluctant to demonstrate any "feminine" attributes.

According to Michael Kaufman, we live in a society that devalues nurturing and emotions, and this may cause us to overlook these characteristics in men.[5] It is important that we focus on emotions and reveal them as a normative part of many men's lives. Men need to be able to learn to talk and emote without women doing that work for us.[6] To do this, we need to be allowed to speak freely, in an environment where everyone understands that what we say could elsewhere be misconstrued because of a lack of vocabulary. We need to build a vocabulary that will allow us to share how we live our gender as men. The men who teach primary grades are a special case example of this general problem.

Judith Cook and Mary Fonow point out that one of their themes of feminist methodology is the centrality of consciousness raising as a specific methodological tool and as a way of seeing.[7] Teachers generally have few opportunities to exchange ideas regarding their teaching, and men teachers, in particular, are especially isolated from others. Amy Richert suggests that women's autobiographies may have been incomplete because they did not want to disclose anything about themselves that flew in the face of definitions of femininity.[8] This is also the case for these men in that they are reluctant to reveal anything about themselves that might appear unmasculine. In an unthreatening environment, however, men, like women, are more likely to freely disclose their true feelings and their perceptions of the problems they face on a daily basis.

Consciousness-raising groups have provided several benefits for women. Participants are more likely to have increased self-esteem, personal and intellectual autonomy, awareness of commonalties, the ability to express feelings such as anger, improved woman-to-woman relationships, and a more highly developed sociopolitical analysis of the female experience and women's experience with oppression. Through consciousness raising, a way of articulating women's standpoints has been created.[9] Because the men in my study are not members of the hegemonic core, their perspective represents a subordinated standpoint. It is not likely that this standpoint will fully develop and emerge in meaningful ways unless the men talk to each other and exchange experiences. Men in general, and men teachers in particular, have not yet had their consciousness raised.[10] While the focus groups were not manifestly consciousness-raising groups, they did provide both a forum for open discussion and an opportunity for an uninvolved witness to observe the dynamics of the men's exchange.

In an intriguing study in England, Mary Thornton organized a men's club to try to alleviate the alarming attrition rate (she calls it "wastage") of men from teacher education programs. She posited that these gatherings might provide an opportunity for men to discuss issues they felt were important and specific to being men in a predominately women's occupation. When the attendance at the scheduled meetings turned out to be rather low, her explanation was that the men might be hesitant to feel vulnerable, might assume they didn't need such a support mechanism, or simply wanted to subvert the "rules" in traditional masculine fashion. A disconcerting conclusion on her part was that having a woman faculty member organize and facilitate the sessions was not likely a factor in the low participation.[11] Thornton's interpretations of men's behaviors are traditional and stereotypical. The men don't just *feel* vulnerable; they *are* vulnerable. While they may realize the value of a support mechanism, they refrain from doing anything to call more attention to themselves. Like other tokens, they prefer to stay out of the limelight. Assuming the men want to subvert the rules is blatant gender bias and contributes to some of the difficulties men teachers must face. Last, the findings of my study clearly indicate that discussing the major issues in men teachers' lives is a potential minefield because of the lack of precise language with which to communicate ideas. The men learn early, from myriad sources, that attempts at explaining their lived experiences as an occupational minority are either met with outright dismissal or contribute to the level of suspicion under which they must operate. One needs only to read the conclusions arrived at in Thornton's study to see how easily stereotypical views of masculinity can uncritically slip into an inquiry into men's lives.

Cultural Fit

Jill Nelson describes a corporate culture in which people can feel various levels of discomfort because of being different or because they experience some form of internal contradiction or "bind," thus finding themselves segregated.[12]

In addition to the general discomfort the men felt over being under suspicion, other uncomfortable conditions exist. The men described three specific types of situations. The first is when the conversation that is taking place is simply of no interest to them. The men, as Dennis says, have nothing to contribute and so feel left out.

> It's not that I don't get into conversations, but when they're talking about menstrual cramps or going into having hot flashes, or they don't feel as com-

fortable nor do I, and you can tell the conversation
is, "Oh, well a male's here." And they'll actually
say, "Oh, we can't talk because Dennis is here with
us now." Or they get into the male-bashing component. It's just social components; women have their
"girl talk," and if you're sitting in there, you kind
of get in the way of that. Many times they forget
that I'm in there, and they start talking anyway, and
then they'll say, "And what do you think?" That's
good for both of us sometimes. But sometimes it's
just beneficial for them for me not to be in there
during their discussions. It sort of intrudes on their
environment. They're talking about change of life
or their husband's sexual ability or whatever, and
me sitting there, I cramp their style. So I understand that.

John points out the second issue. Many of the men often feel
that anything they attempt to contribute will be dismissed as invalid.

And I know lots of people who have a really hard
time because they're the only male. It is a terrible
position to be in. It's very difficult from the perspective that when there's a man you can joke
around and back and forth whatever and you can
talk about some stupid thing, whatever, and you
feel like there's someone like you. But the men that
are by themselves, they feel very much like, like
they're the man. Women often make statements
about "You think this because you think you ARE
the man," and that means that it must be a male
perspective or something like that. It's very difficult for them with the sexual harassment laws that
we have. It's very difficult for some of these people; they've told me they need to get out, because
they're afraid to talk. They're afraid to talk to peo-

ple because if someone takes it the wrong way.
They're afraid to talk to someone in the room after
school with someone. They're afraid that someone
would take it the wrong way.

Finally, Manuel voices the notion that men teachers can be the
targets of women teachers' harassment.

Manuel: I have felt uncomfortable sometimes
when people say sexual comments, where if I was
a female in an all-male group, you could more or
less say it's sexual harassment, but you'd always,
it's not always appropriate to discuss, I don't think
females realize that about males. They expect that
you can handle what you're saying. Like deroga-
tory comments sometimes.

Paul: What kinds of remarks?

Manuel: You know, just sexual jokes sometimes.
Or they talk about their experiences with their hus-
bands, or like those kinds of conversations you
don't need to be hearing at lunchtime.

Because the definition of sexism emerged with the women's
movement, the notion that men can be victims of this same ideology
is not readily accepted. A valid argument could be made that since
women, as a group, lack societal power when compared to men, as
a group, they cannot be guilty of sexism in the form of discrimina-
tory behaviors. The men's use of the term, however, is less precise.
They are simply saying that in the culture of primary teaching, the
majority sets the rules and the norms and the minority must adapt.
Often, the speech and behaviors of the majority are established in
the absence of any input from the minority and may be contrary to
the interests and tastes of the minority. While the men may find
some of the women's statements distasteful, even hurtful, they are

not comfortable protesting. Again, any sign of objection on the part of the men can be taken as an indication of weakness or of demonstrating "feminine" characteristics. This is yet another situation in which the men feel they must remain silent. Their sense that it would be fruitless to complain is supported by studies that indicate that people are not at all sensitive to sexist language directed toward men despite being highly sensitive to sexist language directed toward women.[13]

The men are so involved in avoiding anything that could be construed as feminine that they reproduce the stereotypical masculine presentation of self.[14] In doing so, they inadvertently reproduce gender dichotomy (separate spheres) and the myths about men in teaching. Many of the men feel they are caught in the classic gender bind that is usually associated with women working in predominately male occupations. They feel they have to represent teaching on one hand and men on the other.

The workplace segregation that takes place is sometimes a product of the underrepresentation of men and sometimes an intentional act on the part of the men in reaction to the activities of others.[15] Dennis and Dave, for example, like many men, retreat to their classrooms to eat lunch.

> Dennis: Well, there's a couple ladies that are divorced, and they're in the process of dating and stuff, and so when they get into their "my husband was a jerk" and this business, it's an infringement. I'm sort of sitting there getting all that. Sometimes it's helpful for both of us because they'll ask questions. They go, "Why do you think guys do this?" and we have these really good discussions about male and female. But when they want to have fun about making fun or knocking men and putting them down, it's not exactly thrilling to be around all the time. I end up being the one that seems to be supporting the male, and I don't want to be doing this all the time so that's why I pull myself out.

*****

Dave: I never go in for lunch anymore. I never go
into lunch, into the lounge, into the staff room
because it's just really, it's tedious.

In most corporate cultures, the women who have taken positions
in predominately male areas find themselves excluded from "shop
talk" when the men go off to the local pub or other typically masculine environments to continue business discussion. In teaching,
while there is no indication of actual strategy sessions being held
after hours, several of the men explained that the women teachers
organized shopping trips, lunches, or exercise or movie outings that
excluded the men while seemingly including any women who over-
heard the plans.

Jake: You know, women teachers, they sometimes
go off campus after school or something. They
might socialize, they might get together on the
weekends or something. I haven't made any real
close friendships with teachers, but I do socialize
when I'm on campus. It's a nice group, too. We
have a really nice staff.

*****

Don: Sometimes when they're talking, I can tell
they're continuing a conversation they had away
from work.

Paul: What's the topic?

Don: Oh, a new district policy, or a kid with problems. The best way to handle it. That kind of thing.

Elisabeth Hansot and David Tyack state that it is often more use-
ful to focus on an institution's policies and practices, rather than on

individuals, when we are interested in determining the salience of gender.[16] But they caution that policies and practices may be implicitly gendered even if explicitly gender-blind, because the practices are so deeply embedded in the institutional culture and have gone unquestioned for so long. Perhaps as men we are not sensitized to seeing gender as a phenomenon that influences our daily lives. By listening carefully to men's narratives, it is apparent that gender is indeed present as an organizing structure in the lives of men elementary school teachers even though they themselves often attest to its absence. They rarely see a connection between their daily struggles as teachers and the rules that affect men and women differently.

Cumulative Effect

James Levine talks about occupational segregation working two ways and "norms of manliness" acting as a psychological barrier to keep men out of traditional female work.[17] This may not go far enough. By focusing only on the psychological barriers, he overlooks the possibility of other, more material barriers that men face. Similarly, Christine Williams poses the idea that women in men's work have to deal with the apparent threat they pose to others while men in women's work must deal with the apparent identity crisis that ensues. She tells us that problems of gender for women are an external issue while for men they are internal.[18] The question this begs is: where would men obtain information that threatens their identity? The men I spoke with make it clear that they are seen as serious threats to others. By saying that there are no real assaults upon men who try to cross over or men who display counter-stereotypical behaviors and values, we may be inadvertently closing off communication with those men who would like to tell us about the difficulties they experience. There is ample evidence in the research regarding men day-care providers to show that much of what they suffer is external.[19] Accusations and suspicions of abuse were the primary problem of men day-care workers. In other words, the men found they were perceived as threats to the children.[20] Levine discovered that people were limited, in their frame of reference, to thinking about men and children only through models of fatherhood,[21] which is not necessarily a positive image when compared to motherhood. Fatherhood, as a cultural metaphor, carries images of the detached financial provider and disciplinarian.[22] Since primary teaching is framed through the metaphor of motherhood, men can't fit this metaphor while simultaneously living up to expectations of hegemonic masculinity.

The men in my study often expressed their perceptions of others' expectations about masculinity in the teaching profession. These perceptions, in turn, partly shape how these men behave, negotiate masculinity, and justify their behaviors. That is, these perceptions shape the way these men do gender.[23] The men in this study actually appear to be doing *genders* while they negotiate a path through contradictory expectations. One gender is hegemonic masculinity, with the men being asked to model dominant masculine roles. However, the job itself, composed of daily interactions with small children, demands that they behave in non-hegemonic ways to accomplish the goals of teaching. The problem is, they can't actually perform teaching the way women do, so they are in danger of, at a minimum, demonstrating ineptness. What the data in this study are showing is that the men are being forced to "do teaching" by doing a kind of safe form of hegemonic masculinity, albeit one that is closely monitored, through the use of compensatory activities. As Rosabeth Moss Kanter's studies show us, minority members who attempt to emulate the majority typically are more likely to increase the majority's distrust than to gain their favor.[24]

The cumulative effect of the men attempting to do these multiple genders is a reproduction of "traditional gender ideologies."[25] While many men are apparently willing to take the step into the world of women and children, the structural impediments to assuming the role of teacher in the same way women would and could are too difficult for individual men to overcome. Arlie Hochschild, in her work, *The Second Shift*, ends a chapter about "new men" with a statement about men who have "yet to embrace a notion of themselves as equally important as their wives at home."

Men like Michael Sherman and Art Winfield lead the way into that third stage of fatherhood. But they've done it privately. They are tokens in the world of new fathers. Lacking a national social movement to support them in a public challenge to the prevailing notion of motherhood, they've acted on their own. Not until the other Michael Shermans and Art Winfields step forward, not until a critical mass of men becomes like them, will we end the painful stall in this revolution all around this."[26]

Sociologist Mike Messner agrees with Hochschild:

One of the most important changes that men could make would be to become more equally involved in parenting. The development of early bonding between fathers and infants (in addition to that between mothers and infants) along with nonsexist childrearing in the family, schools and sports would have far-reaching effects on society: Boys and men could grow up more psychologically secure, more able to develop balance between separation and attachment, more able at an earlier age to appreciate intimate relationships with other men without destructive and crippling competition and homophobia.[27]

He goes beyond the personal decisions that men can make, however.

An analysis of men's lives that simply describes personal changes while taking social structures as a given cannot adequately ask these questions [regarding the relationship between personal changes and "social politics and cultural contexts"].[28]

While I agree with Hochschild's overall plea for more men "stepping forward," my research with men teachers has demonstrated that even when men do cross over, there remains an enormous number of structural issues that must be changed and that are beyond the resources of individual men. In addition, there are clearly obstacles to men even stepping forward, since this entails more than just some show of hands indicating interest. It means risking stigmatization and severe negative sanctions.

The cumulative effect of having extra duties assigned to them, including physical tasks and discipline, being expected to model masculinities that might be foreign to them, operating under constant scrutiny, and feeling generally out of place, does not facilitate the kind of empowerment necessary to make the wholesale changes to which Hochschild alludes.

Other writers have argued that the crossing over of large numbers of men into the women's spheres has not made significant changes in the larger societal system of gender division of labor and gender inequality.[29] This is clearly a weak argument in light of my findings. First, there is no evidence that "large numbers" of men are venturing into women's work, and the small percentage of men who do venture into women's work do so at the risk of being treated differently from other men and from the women in the sphere which they enter. These tokens do not change the social structure they enter but are instead influenced by it, just as women who enter traditionally male spheres do not dramatically change the organizations. Second, given the small numbers of men crossing over, and particularly in light of the gendered structure they are encountering, it seems premature to argue that, since they're crossing over and not changing anything, crossing over is not a credible solution to gender inequality. The logical extension of this argument seems to be that there is no reason to attempt to assist more men in becoming teachers. These arguments lay the responsibility for institutionalized practices squarely on the shoulders of individual men, which is an unrealistic and unfair obligation.

The men are walking a fine line between teaching and masculinity. This could be an example of why masculinity is so important for the men. If their masculinity is questioned, their whole person is in question, including their appropriateness for the world of small children. If they look too feminine, they are morally suspect; if too stereotypically masculine, it is feared that the children will suffer from harm or neglect.

There are also consequences for the school and the students. Men's classrooms may be quite different from women's classrooms. Men's rooms typically contain more of the unruly kids and, therefore, have more of an emphasis on discipline. The rules against touching and other close interactions create the need for many compensatory activities, which contribute to the divergent teaching styles of men and women. Students, particularly boys, may be affected profoundly by these differences by internalizing what appear to be "appropriate" gender behaviors and identities.[30]

> Nate: My real fear is that I'm accidentally teaching
> the boys not to be nurturing. I mean, I'm not being
> nurturing. It's a vicious circle.

According to Jim Allan, the men in his collaborative interviews were aware of doing gender, which he calls a kind of work, and also aware of operating within conflicting stereotypes. The men felt challenged to find the feminine aspects of teaching within themselves while not displaying suspicious activities.[31] Unlike women teachers, the men are being evaluated on two fronts. First, their gender appropriateness, whether they are performing masculinity in an acceptable manner, is an important issue because it is the source of the intense scrutiny that structures their work lives. My own interviews suggest that many men feel they were hired specifically to provide masculinity in the lives of the children. Second, they are evaluated on their teaching effectiveness that, for men, includes some additional gender-specific tasks. These two fronts are interdependent since the occupation is so gendered.

Elisabeth Hansot and David Tyack tell us that "a way of seeing is also a way of not seeing." Traditionally, the androcentric view of education didn't "see" gender. The authors define gender "policies" as explicit rules that apply in different or similar ways to the two sexes. Gender "practices" are customary arrangements or regularities of expected behaviors that have crystallized into patterns that may or may not reflect official policy. They look at schools institutionally, as being organized to help people make a transition to gender relations in other institutions. Schools are also *structured by* other institutions. Gender relations from elsewhere come into schools in the form of taken-for-granted gender expectations. Hansot and Tyack have developed a "map" to evaluate gender relationships in an institution. This map consists of differential access, the degree of physical segregation, the sexual division of labor, the distribution of rewards, and the roles of men and women in shaping and implementing policy.[32] Applying the map to elementary schools, it becomes clear that gender is a powerfully significant device in ordering the lives of primary teachers. In other words, gender may sometimes be as salient for men as for women, but in different ways.[33]

Implications

One of the great problems with putting one's research experience, findings, and conclusions into writing is that it must ultimately take on the appearance of linearity, giving the impression of sequential activities.[34] Research, however, is multi-directional and often backs up, restarts, and changes direction. My research into the lives of men elementary school teachers has been circuitous, somewhat fragmented, and often contradictory. It was also continually enlightening. This is a study that began *about* men teachers. Ultimately it was done *with* and *for* them as well, and it is important because it makes several contributions to existing knowledge.

First, it highlights the benefits of using focus groups in qualitative research. There are implications both for choice of techniques of data gathering and for the interpretation of those data gathered. Second, it provides us with another standpoint (worldview) through which to examine the various manifestations of gender construction—the standpoint of men who favor less dominant forms of masculinity. This standpoint provides new information about the societal division of labor and about some new possibilities for dismantling the gender order by supporting the crossing over of men into activities normally associated with women.

The use of focus groups improved this project in important ways. By using more than one method, I was able to check one piece of data against another knowing that they had been collected at different times and under different conditions. Norman Denzin has labeled this a form of triangulation, a term that implies we view a social scene from multiple viewpoints.[35]

The men themselves validated many of my emerging findings in both direct and indirect ways.[36] They openly stated that my findings and analyses, as presented to them prior to the focus group meetings, reflected a credible account of their experiences and perspectives.

Finally, while I had expected that the men's use of language and their general demeanor would likely change when in the company of other members of their group, I was unprepared for the way that their expressiveness changed, especially over issues of scrutiny and the general culture of the teaching environment. Had I not witnessed the men interacting, I would not have uncovered the hidden resentment and anger over these issues. Without these revelations, many of the other findings would not have had the significance they do. For example, the issue of the men's supposed appropriateness for promotion to administrative positions begins to sound suspiciously like a less than subtle, institutionalized means to coax men away from daily direct contact with the children. In the same way, the daily division of labor now seems less like a matter of personal choice on the men's part and more like an institutionalized sexual division of labor. The idea that the men can feel harassed or discriminated against becomes legitimate when we see that they honestly feel their positions as teachers can be seriously jeopardized if any of their actions or statements are misconstrued. Many of the issues about which they have the most concern are issues that the men perceive as non-negotiable, given the current climate of concern over men's potential danger to children. Their silence regarding these issues could be mistaken for tacit agreement and endorsement. In these focus groups, many of the men felt safe to break their silence and, in presenting their own feelings, discovered that other men felt the same.

Men comprise less than two percent of the teachers in the primary grades. This low participation rate has attracted other researchers and myself.[37] We all wanted to see how men negotiate their masculinities when doing women's work. The more we know about these previously unexamined relations, the more we can contribute to a feminist reconstruction of society.[38] What we were searching for were glimpses into the ways a subordinate masculinity gets done when bound to institutional life, what Robert Connell calls "local accounts of masculinity."[39]

How can we increase the likelihood that bringing men's subjective experiences to light will contribute to the feminist goal of dismantling gender? Harry Brod proposes we study non-hegemonic men in respect to their relations with women and with hegemonic masculinity. In so doing we are likely to discover the "sort of double bind [that] is precisely characteristic of gender norms in non-hegemonic cultures."[40] His specific discovery was that Jewish men have to make a choice between aligning with Jewish women or with hegemonic masculinity. bell hooks describes the same type of bind for Black women in that they are in danger of losing the support of Black men in their fight against racism if they align with white women to fight sexism.[41] Men elementary teachers tread a similar fine line, and their stories reveal how complex and perilous these ambiguities can be.

These men's stories are not well known yet, but this is not unusual. The knowledge produced by marginalized groups is typically suppressed so that the dominant group can view the subordinate as a willing participant in its own marginalization. Self-defined standpoints are suppressed because they can stimulate resistance against dominant images (e.g., disciplinarian, effeminate) that have provided ideological justification for oppression. Self-naming is subversive, and dominant groups have a vested interest in continuously suppressing such thought.[42] But standpoint isn't just about how "they" think—it is about adding to the ways we *all* should think. We need new ways of knowing—ones that will allow subordinate groups to define their *own* reality and thus create empowerment.

Standpoint is an achieved perspective that comes out of the struggle between the hegemonic group in control of an ideology and those who must live by it. This struggle is revealed in the societal division of labor that puts children into the exclusive care of women, both in the home and in more social venues such as day care and elementary schools.[43]

A feminist critique of traditional science consists of the need for many additional standpoints through which to do our inquiries.[44] "Let's be more inclusive by incorporating the experiences and perspectives of traditionally excluded groups."[45] If we center the experiences of the marginalized, we decrease the likelihood of ignoring their perspective. Michael Messner provides these instructions for those interested in men and masculinity as a line of inquiry:

> From whose standpoint can we develop a more true understanding of men and masculinity?... From the point of view of those who advocate a feminist standpoint, men who study masculinity should be attempting to help break the circle of the conventional social production of patriarchal knowledge.[46]

Messner's instruction doesn't imply that we must ignore our experiences or abandon the theories we formulate as men. Messner continues later, "To the contrary, it is precisely our experiences as men and our access to masculine worlds that give us the potential to construct a powerful critique of masculinity." Messner then adds the point that, in producing knowledge, men must "check with women."[47] The most effective way to check with women, and with other men, is to publish these findings in a way that authentically presents the perspective of the men themselves.

In the first chapter, I presented Scott Coltrane's suggestions for incorporating men's standpoints into gender studies. He suggests that we focus on men's emotions, study the men's groups to which we, as men, have access, and put men's experiences into a structural context. He also suggests we look into the lives of men who are involved in activities traditionally thought of as women's.[48] In these activities gender—specifically masculinity—will be made most visible because of the strains involved in negotiating a gender identity that is in conflict with institutional definitions.[49]

When we consider the strong possibility that there are multiple genders, and not just two, we have to account for several masculinities and femininities and the relations among them. The men who come to teaching come to the profession doing a subordinate masculinity in terms of their desire to be close to children, to nurture, and to pursue alternative modes of success, and they come with a worldview that possibly emphasizes process over goals. These are values that are recognized as traditionally feminine and have been devalued economically and politically.

While they may not clearly spell out any strategy for actively dismantling the gender order, the men teachers often reveal their efforts to negotiate through a variety of socially constructed expectations while continuously reconstructing their masculinities. Though perhaps not gender revolutionaries, they are clearly fighting a quiet battle.[50] On one hand, they are fighting to prove they are real teachers—just as women must fight to prove they are real police officers.[51] On the other, they must also continually prove that they are real men, as defined by the institutionalized practices and policies of the teaching profession. Underlying this already complex dynamic is the men's need to constantly prove they are not a danger to the children. It is this need, more than any, which spawns the series of creative compensatory activities that facilitate the men's precarious balancing act. The presence of these compensatory activities and the intense scrutiny that produces them are the centerpiece of this study. For men teachers several contradictory demands converge, and the men must work to remain balanced.

The social control aspect of the scrutiny theme is extremely important. This is an area of powerful overlap with the larger, societal division of labor. While much work has been devoted to ferreting out the mechanisms that act to obstruct women's entrance into male fields, little attention has been paid to what could be seen as a set of potent "back-up" or supportive mechanisms that obstruct men's entrance into women's fields. Using Barbara Reskin's conflict approach, I contend that it does not serve the ends of capitalism (patriarchy) for men to be seen as appropriate caregivers.[52]

At some point in my research, I began writing "voluntary non-hegemony" in the margins of transcripts and notes. It became a metaphor representing the standpoint of men who do women's work—men are exerting continual energy into distancing themselves from patriarchal power. Christine Williams' metaphor of the escalator, while graphically depicting the men's constant state of moving to stay in place, begs the question of whose definition of the situation is represented by the "up" direction of the escalator.[53] After speaking with these men, I would be more likely to envision a fast-moving river in which the men are forced to swim vigorously just to stay abreast of their women peers. If they cease their efforts, they could easily be swept to other locales—pleasant places, perhaps, but not ones of the men's choosing.

Jim Allan's metaphor of "anomaly" is disturbing in that he seems to take at face value that the men who choose to do women's work are "exceptions."[54] In terms of demographics, this is correct. However, it may be confusing effect for cause, and we may be further contributing to the image of men as generally unsuited for child care if we too easily accept the *a priori* notion that men who are good with and for children are rare. How do we know until we have looked into all the ways men similar to those in my study have been silenced? One of the most distinctive characteristics of stereotypes is that they endure despite empirical evidence that contradicts them. Group members who present in ways counter to stereotypical views are quickly categorized as exceptions to the rule, as are tokens in an organization. Many tokens, however, adopt the behaviors they perceive are expected of them by the dominant group.[55] Even more important, members of an underrepresented group will often espouse the rhetoric of the dominant group in declaring that they (the non-exceptional members of the underrepresented group) are unfit for the positions held by the exceptional token.[56]

On the surface, many of the men teachers I interviewed did seem to support the idea that they saw themselves as exceptions in terms of being safe for children, while men in general should be considered dangerous. However, in light of the findings that show this to be common among groups who are in the minority in an organization, I argue that a close inspection of the total picture that emerges from the interviews is needed.[57] To the problem I posed regarding increasing the number of men in teaching, twenty-six of the thirty-five men proposed plans that exposed teaching as appropriate men's work to the male population in general. Nowhere in their narratives was there any mention of screening, such as that suggested by Christine Skelton.[58] Only four men expressed reservations about increasing the number of men, and their concerns included reservations about the quality of both men and women teachers along several dimensions. Five other men were ambivalent as demonstrated by their lack of any suggestions for action. Almost half the men preferred "affirmative action" steps. These suggestions do not reflect the stance of men who feel the general population of men is dangerous for children.

A theme of "better safe than sorry" runs through the narratives of the men teachers, the policies and practices they describe, and the literature regarding the issue of men in early teaching. Like other marginalized groups described by Jill Nelson, men teachers are careful not to draw attention to themselves by deviating too much from the narrow parameters of behavior that are circumscribed by the roles they are expected to play.[59] Doing so may mark them as different and, for men in elementary teaching, being different often means being perceived as threatening.[60] Understanding this makes it easy to conclude that the men who teach small children would likely participate in the ongoing construction of "those men out there" as dangerous.

Upon entering women's work, men may indeed be deficient in many of the areas that comprise the job. Men must learn the skills and behaviors that are considered natural for women.[61] Of course, men's deficiencies (compared to women) in the ability to care for and nurture children, to be there for them, are not natural, but the result of what Jerry Jacobs calls "cumulative disadvantage." This consists of a life-long series of experiences, socially prescribed, that prepare men and women for the roles they are expected to fulfill as adults.[62] Janet Lever calls this "anticipatory socialization"; it clearly resembles the notion of the "self-fulfilling prophecy."[63] Theodore Cohen and Scott Coltrane both demonstrate that men learn to care for children through practice, through using their bodies in new ways and feeling the sensations associated with holding infants and being in physical contact with children.[64] These, too, are new standpoints that have been too long unheard.

> They don't tell you what it's like to hold the
>   naked body of your child fresh from the bath.
> There's no "Father's School" to instruct you in
>   the joy of a wet and squirming, then dry and
>   incredibly soft little bottom.
> Only mothers pass on the folklore surrounding
>   that joy.
> Fathers are merely told of pride when the kid gets
>   to school or the football team or the roll call of
>   dead veterans.
> I can only anguish at all the joy I missed, all the
>   closeness I avoided because of the embarrass-
>   ment at touching the nakedness of my infants.
> No one taught me one could be intimate without
>   being sexual.
> And now suddenly my babies are grown to be
>   men, knowing how to be a father only from me.
> I'm sorry boys. So sorry.
> But no one told me.[65]

In the moving words of poet Robert Anderson we can hear the pain associated with realizing that as men we have accepted the belief that our place in the lives of children is profoundly different—more distant and removed—from that of women. Too often, the realization that things could be otherwise comes too late, and we wish that we had been provided with a different image of masculinity to guide us. The men in my study are sources of an alternate view of men, and by graciously participating in this study they are telling us about it.

~ 7 ~

The Research: A Personal and Professional Odyssey

In the course of this life I have had a great many encounters with a great many people who have been concerned with matters of consequence. I have lived a great deal among grown-ups. I have seen them intimately, close at hand. And that hasn't much improved my opinion of them.

Whenever I met one of them who seemed to me at all clear-sighted, I tried the experiment of showing them my Drawing Number One, which I have always kept. I would try to find out, so, if this was a person of true understanding. But, whoever it was, he, or she, would always say:

"That is a hat."

Then I would never talk to that person about boa constrictors, or primeval forests, or stars. I would bring myself down to his level. I would talk to him about bridge, and golf, and politics, and neckties. And the grown-up would be greatly pleased to have met such a sensible man.

— From *The Little Prince*
by Antoine de Saint Exupery (1941/1971)

In his classic critique of modernity, *The Little Prince*, Antoine de Saint Exupery tells of his childhood experiences as a budding artist. After being enthralled by photos from a book describing the primeval forest, he set pencil to paper and drew a picture of a boa constrictor that had eaten its prey, an elephant, whole and was settling down to digest it. Unfortunately, each adult he showed his picture to thought the image was a man's hat. Eventually his parents convinced him to give up this inconsequential pastime and pursue more fitting (masculine?) activities. He never stopped carrying the old drawing around, though, in hopes that he would one day show it to someone who would recognize it for what it was intended to mean. This person, then, would be one who could truly comprehend him and perhaps share his perspective of how the world operates.[1]

We are far more likely to speak openly to those who have indicated that they understand our worldview. That is why, as researchers, we make a concerted effort to see the world through the participants' system of meaning, to practice a form of Max Weber's *verstehen* and truly learn to see the world as another sees it.[2]

I selected qualitative research methods because I did not know specifically what I was looking for and because I wanted to generate data rich in detail and embedded in context. My goal from the outset was to discover how the gendered division of labor is defined from the perspective of the actors. For this reason I chose in-depth interviewing, or ethnographic interviewing.[3] To paraphrase Ann Oakley, I wanted to talk with men about the very personal business of being male in a predominately female occupation.[4] Clyde Franklin and Michael Kimmel are among those who call for new ways of deeply penetrating the surface of men's lives.[5] I wanted to pose questions to men that are more often posed to women about their experiences entering and remaining in gender-atypical occupations. Susan Bell and Marilyn Yalom advise us that men are less likely than women to see themselves as gendered. At least they do not see gender as an organizing force in their lives.[6] Men may not see themselves as doing gender but as simply living up to societal expectations. Or, to adapt Herbert Blumer's term, perhaps gender is not a "sensitizing concept" for men.[7]

This lack of sensitivity to gender made me aware of the extra demands that would be put on me as a researcher. I would have to probe for areas that would reveal the way that gender affects these men harder than I might have to with women, yet without tainting the responses by verbally leading them into areas of my choosing. This idea of the "absence" of gender from men's lives pervades the entire research process.

In the remainder of this chapter I will first outline locating and recruiting the participants. Next, I will describe the interview process itself, including the focus groups. I will then explain the steps I followed in analyzing the transcripts of the interviews and my field journal. Finally, I will present my reasons for writing this work the way in which I did. I will also include the ethical considerations that affected the study. As with most qualitative projects, these steps were not separate and linear.

The Participants

My strategy for locating participants was straightforward. I used a directory published by the local Office of Education (a public document available to anyone who wishes to purchase it) to determine the school addresses of men teachers. I then sent them personal letters at their respective school addresses.

At the end of each interview, I asked each participant for the names of any other men teachers. My original target was to interview thirty K-6 teachers. Soon, though, I changed my focus to K-3 because it is at these grade levels that men are most underrepresented. I believe that my study actually expanded rather than narrowed when I focused on the primary grades even though I was looking at fewer grades. This is because I was able to concentrate my probing on the minutiae of the daily lives of these men without having to consider the clearly different job tasks that are included in teaching the older children.

The directory I used listed 146 elementary schools with a total enrollment of 95,800 students within the districts I targeted. The proportion of men principals and teachers throughout the districts is presented in the following table.

Number of schools 146
Percent men principals 30
Number of K-6 teachers 3,444
Number of K-6 teachers who are men 309 (9%)
Number of K-3 teachers 2,002
Number of K-3 teachers who are men 61 (3%)

Since I am interested in the experiences associated with long-term relationships with children, I focused only on regular class-room teachers, omitting resource, dedicated bilingual, and special education teachers.

One of my aims in sampling was to increase the diversity of my sample as much as possible along race, class, sexuality, experience, marital, and family status parameters. This goal was not entirely within my control since I can only draw from the total population of men currently employed in the districts' primary grade classrooms. My objective, however, was diversity, rather than some kind of representativeness. I ultimately interviewed thirty-five men. I re-interviewed four of the men, and six of them participated in two focus groups of three persons each. These thirty-five men represent almost sixty percent of the total number of men teaching K-3 in the districts within which I recruited.

The men's ages ranged from early 20s to late 50s. Twenty-two are married, and all the married men except four have children. The range of teaching experience is from one to over thirty years. Most have been teaching about nine years (the median and mean). To my question, "How would you identify yourself ethnically?" four men said "African American," two "Black," two "Japanese American," one "Vietnamese American," five "Mexican American," one "Latino," seventeen "white," two "Irish," and one "Caucasian."

In response to my initial open-ended question regarding their path into teaching, all of the men began their narratives by providing a brief description of their families of origin. In all but six cases, the men describe a middle-class family of origin. This means that they presented a picture of a family who lived in comfortable homes, enjoyed a stable family life, and were active in the community. The men's parents were described as having high aspirations for the men in terms of education and career advancement. In most cases the men also described a comfortable standard of living in which they wanted for little.[8]

Six men (two Black, one Mexican American, and three white) described a working-class background in which their parents were employed in a trade or service job and were typically pressed for resources to make ends meet. The three minority men in this group also referred to their ethnic identification as being contributory to their personal experiences as teachers. They were the only ones of the eighteen non-white men who did so.

The Interviews

To provide for the comfort of the participants, I offered to conduct the interviews in a location of their choosing. Nine interviews were in the participants' homes, seven at local coffee shops, thirteen in the men's classrooms after school, and six in my office on campus. Both the focus groups were conducted in a small conference room on campus.

The interviews were tape-recorded and transcribed. Interviews began with an open-ended question such as, "Tell me about getting into teaching." Subsequent questions flowed from my list of prompts designed to elicit rich detail. Other questions were framed around what problems the participants encountered in the course of their work lives.[9]

Each initial interview lasted approximately 60 to 90 minutes. I asked each participant for permission to return if I needed to clarify or expand on responses. I ensured that my questions, demeanor, and interview style framed the conversations in egalitarian terms. Interviews, in other words, were conversational, non-hierarchical, and based in an ethic of caring.[10] My own stance reflected a kind of naive ignorance, inviting them to teach me about their lives. The idea was to catch men in what would not typically be considered routine stances in terms of what they say, how they say it, and who among them express which issues. There is much said about men's lack of emotionality and expressiveness in interviews. It is possible that this is over-generalized, and I went into the project challenging such stereotypes and assuming for the moment that the stereotypes are not true. Instead, I took my lead from Theodore Cohen, Mitch Duneier, and Michael Messner, who report that the men in their research projects enjoyed the opportunity to tell how they felt about the events in their lives once trust and rapport were established.[11]

I wanted to listen keenly to what aspects of teaching the men emphasized. I expressed respect for, and concern about, these men by learning about them, their perspective, and their world, and by being personally involved.[12] Norman Denzin offers the idea of the "interpretive interactional approach." The basic question is how people live and give meaning to lives and capture these meanings in written, narrative, and oral forms.[13] Robert Traver says narrative has long been a way to measure our culture. There is a kind of generalizability that comes out of sharing stories and finding the commonalties that may exist.[14] One of my challenges was to help men give voice to their lives in ways they have not done before.

Following Elliott Mishler, I ensured that there was a definite circularity to the interviews. Each successive question or probe was grounded in a previous response from the participant.[15] As Carol Gilligan demonstrated, we can't simply ask a question and then code the answer as though there was only one way for the question (and answer) to be understood.[16] Meaning is jointly constructed. Informants may have a great deal of difficulty understanding our questions and may require a few attempts on our part to ask the questions. Mishler admits he was prone to deciding that an informant's response was inappropriate for the question asked and would try to redirect the informant. To avoid this, I simply assumed that the answer was correct from the respondent's perspective and used the analysis (coding) stage to determine what it was the respondent decided I had asked.

Charles Briggs discovered that interviewing errors are seldom reported. With all our accrued knowledge about interviews, we still know very little about them as communication events. We take interviews for granted, in other words. Interviews are, however, problematic. First, they are "metacommunication" in that they give participants a notion of the communication rules that are being imposed at the time. These rules are, more often than not, contrary to the prevailing metacommunication rules in place in the general culture. Second, interviews create the stereotypical roles of interviewer and interviewee of which most of us have direct or indirect knowledge. Third, the prevailing communication norms of the culture cannot be screened out entirely. Following Briggs's suggestions, I examined the transcripts of interviews for any indication that the teachers and I had misunderstood each other. When I found these instances, I deferred to the teachers' meaning system.[17] Had I been faithful to my interview guide, I would have been more assertive in structuring the questions, including the order in which I asked them, and insisting the teachers provide "best" answers.

I was constantly on the alert for the teachers' definition of the interview situation itself. Since they had all completed extensive post-secondary education, they were all familiar with the scientific process. The perception of "normal science" on the teachers' part affected their notion of what rules were in play. They often responded in terms of causes, as demonstrated by their desire to know what I was trying to *prove*. One thing in my favor is that I asked teachers to teach me, so there wasn't an insurmountable gap between their communicative norms and that of the interview.

Analysis of Transcripts

Analyzing the interview data was an ongoing process. I identified many of the emerging themes during the transcription process itself, although some were taken from the existing literature and from my previous research, what Matthew Miles and Michael Huberman would call a "start list." In general, I followed the grounded theory approach with some of the particular techniques coming from James Spradley's Developmental Research Sequence.[19] By using Spradley's framework and the coding logic of grounded theory,[20] I found the process lent itself well to computer-aided analysis. Memoing, categorizing, and theorizing can be accomplished from within the program, and these become further data for analysis. Subsequent interview transcripts are added according to the "constant comparison" method of Barny Glaser and Anselm Strauss. This means that all interview transcripts are re-analyzed upon the addition of each new transcript.[21]

Focus Groups

I asked every teacher if he would agree to participate in a focus group interview. Although most said they would, it was also clear that actually finding the time would be difficult. Ultimately, it was possible to schedule six men to participate in two separate sessions. Although other men expressed a desire to participate, it was not possible to synchronize their schedules. The meetings took place in a conference room allowing all of us to sit around a table making for easy eye contact with each of the other participants. Prior to the meeting, each of the men had had a chance to review a rough draft of the themes that I had perceived as emerging from the stories. Some of the themes were fairly well developed, and I had embedded them in existing literature. The following themes were presented in my draft to the men:

- The men felt constantly under scrutiny around the children.
- They were ambivalent about being male role models.
- Promotions were not seen as an important career objective.
- Women peers were not always supportive.
- There is a distinct division of labor by gender.

- Increasing the number of men in teaching is complex.

I attempted to make the sessions as informal as possible and also relied on the men themselves to build the agenda as they went. I told them they were welcome to come to the session prepared to critique my work, ask me questions about my methods or interpretations, or simply to discuss their reactions to my findings. In both sessions, after introductions, the men immediately began discussing the idea that the themes I had presented were remarkably widespread, yet each man had not really discussed these issues extensively with anyone before speaking with me. As Frank stated, "I was amazed at how many men also felt this way."

There is always the danger that our resulting analysis will have no meaning for the participants. The focus interviews gave me considerable insight into how best to frame my final project to increase its usefulness for the men themselves.[22] The participants unanimously confirmed that my findings were valid and that the issues I had identified are important in their lives. While every man had obviously given much private thought to the issues, each had assumed that the problems were individual, detached from the structure of teaching itself.

In the opening moments of the sessions, the teachers tended to defer to me as the expert who had discovered important components of their lives. Interestingly, the men didn't even acknowledge recognizing their own words in the quotes I provided. As the focus groups progressed, they also heard the other men's statements and confirmed the themes with each other, in their own words. This group validation confirmed that the teachers were using their frame of reference and communicative norms rather than being persuaded to use mine, which would be what Charles Briggs terms "communicative hegemony."[23]

At the outset of each interview, I used the findings section to establish the context for the informants.[24] As quickly as possible, I tried to turn the discussion from the general to the specific, with each man encouraged to share anecdotal evidence.[25] My own role was as facilitator rather than interviewer. The groups were tape-recorded, the tapes transcribed, and the transcripts, like those of the single informant interviews, became both a new source of data and a new point of reference from which to view the data. All of the major themes I am presenting in this research were confirmed to be in customary use in terms of being frequent, widespread, and collective.[26]

The men also engaged in dialogue with each others' ideas, rather than with my presentation of their lives. As David Wellman observed, the men were "forced to confront and disagree with each other and be able to approach issues without being overly concerned with researcher reactions." In this way, my presence was diluted and the men engaged in "humanly meaningful encounters."[27]

Writing

In qualitative projects, the writing phase often begins immediately. In formulating the research puzzle we begin to write about our suspicions, hunches, and any experiences we have had that could possibly relate to the emerging puzzle. Like many qualitative researchers, I began from the outset to keep a journal. In it, I recorded my thoughts, plans, problems, errors, speculations, doubts, and questions. This became an excellent source of insight into my own evolving values and perspective. It is very important for researchers to do this since we, the researchers, *are* the research instruments and, as such, we need to be aware of how our values influence our choices during data collection, analysis, and interpretation.

My personal journal allowed me to examine the kinds of meaning systems I employed at various stages of the project. I also gained valuable insight into ways I have been changed by this process and what kind of researcher was emerging. This personal dimension through which we pay attention to the changing self, the substantive concerns of the research project, and the methods we use is an important issue for fieldworkers.[28] As I stated in my preface, I went into this project with a certain uneasy sense of my feminist self and finished with a slightly different and more coherent one.

My relationship with the various feminisms might be considered ambivalent by many, but I believe that I share a common goal with other feminists in terms of wanting to work toward disassembling the gender order. As Harry Brod points out, however, the particulars of the journey to this goal may be different for men.[29] Those of us who choose to study men and masculinity must keep the needs and perspectives of women in sight, yet somehow we must simultaneously identify the specific details of men's lives that must change to accomplish a reconstitution of society into a more egalitarian one. I went into this project with a general belief that there are men who live lives that do not support patriarchal structure and ideology. I suspect that men who stay home with their children, men who reject conventional standards of success, and men who work in typically women's jobs may be sources of some of the particulars for which we should be searching. Most of these men have placed themselves into a position of voluntary non-hegemony by the choices they have made. It would be instructive to determine the reasons why, and the methods by which, voluntarily non-hegemonic men resist or reject sharing in the patriarchal power that is available to them. Perhaps even more interesting might be the discovery of mechanisms that the men perceive as preventing them from more openly rejecting patriarchy. It has been my contention for many years—since my earliest encounters with feminist standpoints—that giving up power has costs for men that go beyond the obvious decrease in privilege. Negative sanctions in terms of others' suspicions about the men's lack of responsibility and drive or in terms of evoking homophobic reactions can prevent men from outwardly expressing anti-patriarchal ideas.[30] This combination has informed my perspective and, therefore, my research all along. Prior to this research project I did not have the vocabulary to describe my thoughts and feelings about this ambivalence. Once I was aware of my values regarding this issue, I put myself on guard to ensure that these values were not biasing my research by looking for heroes where they don't exist. Additionally, I remained on guard for any possibility of my trivializing any complaints or fears the men expressed.

Reflections on these values and beliefs provided me the opportunity to assess the effect of my values and perspectives on my rapport with the teachers; on my formulation of interview queries and prompts; on my initial, focused, and special coding throughout the analysis of the transcripts; and ultimately on the themes that I chose to use to organize the publication of my findings. It is important to know why some themes are included in the final report and not others. Any observer can come to a setting and "find illustrative material for already extant stereotypes."[31] I will address this issue of themes more fully below.

Another issue that occurred to me as I began my earliest writing about masculinities was the question of pronoun usage when referring generally to men, men's activities, or men's feelings. If I use "they" to speak of men, I seem to appear distant, above, or outside the reality of masculinities. As a man, I often feel that it is more appropriate to use "we" when I believe the readers should be reminded that the author is a member of the group being discussed. Other times, like David Buchbinder, I prefer "they" to avoid any false impression of personal "coziness," such as when I am writing of experiences unique to those men in my sample.[32]

Language use also became an issue when I realized that I was consistently referring to the men as *male* elementary teachers. As I scanned feminist works written about women in traditional male occupations, it was more common for the authors to use "women" workers, not "female" workers. Robert Connell writes,

> It is remarkable how many passages of contemporary writing about sexual politics talk of women as "women" and men as "males." I have never found the reverse.[33]

I decided to use "men" and "women" whenever the syntax would allow. It is peculiar how the term "men elementary teachers" seemed to stick on my tongue at first, while "women engineers" flowed smoothly. After many uses, however, the distinction between them diminished, though it never entirely disappeared. Clearly, there is still much to be written on these topics.

The readers of an ethnography or other qualitative projects need to have a sense that they are seeing the social scene under study through the eyes of a credible "I-witness." This can happen only if the readers are presented with a convincing "I."[34] Throughout my presentation of findings, wherever I have felt it would be meaningful for the reader, I have included statements regarding my own self-reflection. It is likely that I did this as much for my own benefit as for the readers', since it is important that I keep in touch with my own evolving authoritative stance. It is difficult to tread along the thin line that separates the authoritative, or privileged, position of author and the position of the uncritical reporter of the participants' unedited stories. As Nel Noddings warns, it is extremely easy to fall into the habits of normal science in taking an authoritative stance.[35] However, because this is a social science project, it is crucial that I ultimately take responsibility for the analysis—the linking of the lived experience of the men to social theories. The analogy that comes to my mind is that of the relationship between artist and model. While the participants/subjects might well be invited to portray themselves to the researcher/artist in the manner they believe most representative of their real lives, we cannot also hand them the brush and palette. As a researcher, I am responsible for what appears on my canvas from the overall effect through the mixing of the colors to the finest brush strokes.

I have some sense that my work has credibility in the eyes of the participants since more than a dozen of them read my work-in-progress and deemed it representative of their experiences rather than a representation that I created through my choice of words and context.[36] My confidence in the idea that my participants viewed my presentation as having been written *for* them as well as *with* them and *about* them remains high. This is an issue of ethics as well as credibility.

My ethical responsibilities became clear at the outset. Some early findings indicated that many of the responses from these men could put them at risk in their employment. First, some are quite critical of the administration of the school in general. Second, like employees in other bureaucracies, many have opted to operate outside what they define as overly rigid, constraining, and unproductive work rules. Third, almost all are fearful that some portions of what they have to say may be misconstrued by administrators, peers, parents of children, or the public. For these reasons, I have taken all necessary precautions to ensure that the comments these men made to me cannot be linked to them in any way. All identifiers have been purged from the report prior to publication. I have used pseudonyms for all the informants and for any persons referred to by name. In addition, I have used none of the actual names of the institutions or locations in my report.

Since my approach throughout the project was to ask the men to teach me what they believe I should know in order to understand them, I am confident that these are accurate representations of the essence of their thoughts and feelings on these topics. The themes came up over and over and, as Robert Coles says, they began to ring true.[37]

This research has answered many of the questions that were raised early on (see p. 23):

- There are definitely structures and practices that act to obstruct men's entrance into the occupation.
- There are practices that make men's longevity in the profession problematic.
- The culture of early education is gendered (feminized) to the point that men find it difficult to fit in.
- Once inside the occupation, men encounter strong resistance to them teaching in the same way that women teach.
- The men are hesitant to speak openly about most of these issues for fear of exacerbating the already oppressive scrutiny under which they must operate.

As in most research endeavors, several important issues were raised but not answered or resolved satisfactorily. These are now legitimate starting points for future research topics. For example, we need to know more about the experiences of men as they pursue their teaching credentials. Early findings suggest that men may be tracked away from early childhood education and into more appropriately masculine areas. This is the focus of my current research, some of which I have included in this work.

All the men and most of the literature point to a dramatic difference between men's and women's life-long experiences with children and child care. More exploration into this disparity is needed. Why, for example, would parents choose to leave younger siblings in the care of the oldest daughter rather than an even older son?

Overall, the same gendered societal division of labor that finds women facing resistance and, at times, hostility when they attempt to enter traditionally men's spheres also produces obstacles to men crossing into the activities normally associated with women, especially activities involving contact with children. If men cannot care for children on an equal basis with women, then women will continue to be saddled with dual obligations.

We need to understand, from the men's point of view, the structural impediments to men entering and remaining in women's work. Correcting men's dramatic underrepresentation in elementary education is not a simple question of inducing or compelling men to cross over. It is a matter of allowing and assisting them to do so.

Notes

Notes for the Preface

1. As I will explain in my research addendum, I adopted the term "men teachers" rather than "male teachers" because it is more in line with the recent literature that focuses on "women engineers, women police officers, women faculty" and others, instead of "female." The use of "men" and "women" highlights that we are interested in the cultural aspects (gender) of these people's lives, not their biological sex.

2. J. Spradley (1979). *The ethnographic interview*; see also his 1980 companion work, *Participant observation*.

3. M. Wollstonecraft (1792/1983). *A vindication of the rights of woman*, p. 219, for her discussion on thinking and writing in non-linear fashion.

Notes for Chapter One

1. W. F. Whyte (1981), pp. 292-293.

2. According to the National Center for Education Statistics (NCES), (1996).

3. All names of people and places are pseudonyms. I have tried to purge all identifiers.

4. For a description of the ways that service jobs are "gendered," see R. Leidner (1991), "Serving Hamburgers and Selling Insurance:

Gender, Work, and Identity in Interactive Service Jobs."

5. R. Connell (1987), *Gender and power*, p. 183. The important point in his work is that there are multiple genders rather than simply two (i.e., masculine and feminine) that correspond to the biological categories (i.e., male and female).

6. G. Rubin (1975). A "sex/gender system" is a network of interacting institutions, practices, and norms.

7. W. I. Thomas and D. Thomas (1929). The work of William I. Thomas had a dramatic impact on the field of sociology (social psychology). His introduction of the concept, "definition of the situation" has alerted us to the fact that each social actor brings a particular definition to each social scene. Our task is not so much to prove or disprove that definition, but to accept it for what it is: the actor's perspective, which explains the actor's decisions.

8. See R. Connell (1987). *Gender and power*. This is an example of his "theory of embedding," whereby a social system such as gender can establish links with unconscious mental processes and thus gain mass support regardless of its irrationality and destructiveness (see p. 201).

9. A. Lorde (1984), *Sister outsider*.

10. This "performative" view of gender can be found in J. Butler's (1990) *Gender trouble, feminist theory and psychoanalytic discourse*; C. West & D. Zimmerman (1987), "Doing Gender," explain "doing" as legitimating social arrangements based on sex category by linking the "institutional and interactional levels" (p. 147).

11. C. West & D. Zimmerman (1987), "Doing gender," p. 146.

12. See R. Connell (1992), "A very straight gay"; also see his *Masculinities* (1995). He suggests that when people operate outside normal gender expectations, it is possible that the expectations themselves will often be questioned, rather than the behaviors of the social actors.

13. M. W. Shelley (1818/1963), *Frankenstein*, p.147.

14. C. E. Robinson (1976), *Mary Shelley: Collected tales and stories*; see in particular "The heir of Mondolfo" and "The elder son."

15. M. Wollstonecraft (1792/1983), *A vindication of the rights*

of woman; see her "conversation" with Rousseau regarding the need for educating both Emile and his sister Sophie, pp. 56-66.

16. S. E. Martin (1980), *Breaking and entering: Policewomen on patrol*, p. 108. See also "Women scientists and engineers: Trends in participation," by B. M. Vetter (1981); *Breaking the glass ceiling: Can women reach the top of America's largest corporations?* by A. Morrison, R. White, and E. Van Velsor (1987); *Women lawyers: Rewriting the rules,* by M. Harrington (1995); and "An officer and a lady: Organizational barriers to women working as correctional officers in men's prisons" by N. Jurik (1995).

17. J. Hearn (1992), "The personal, the political, the theoretical," p. viii; see also H. Brod (1987), *The making of masculinities: The new men's studies*; and M. Kimmel and M. Messner (1998), *Men's lives*, p. xiii.

18. H. Brod (1987), *The making of masculinities: The new men's studies*, p. 6; see also C. F. Epstein (1991), "It's all in the mind: Personality and social structure"; and R. Connell (1995), *Masculinities*.

19. H. Bradley (1993). "Across the great divide: The entry of men into 'women's jobs.'"

20. H. Brod (1987), A critique of "patriarchy" is, by definition, a critique of a system of relations among men rather than an analysis of the experiences of particular men; see p. 61.

21. D. Morgan (1992), *Discovering men*; B. Thorne (1993), *Gender play*. Both authors caution us to be cognizant that gender is not the only factor at work in a social scene and may not even be the salient issue influencing an actor's life at a given moment. Age, race, class, accent, etc., can all affect how one is perceived and treated.

22. S. Coltrane (1989), *Household labor and the routine production of gender*; R. Connell (1995), *Masculinities*; C. W. Mills (1961), *The sociological imagination*. It is not always easy to conceptualize both the individual and the social system simultaneously, but we must do so if we are to make sense of an individual's experience within the system. Too much emphasis on the individual disregards social forces, while an absolute focus on societal institutions overlooks human agency.

23. b. hooks (1992), *Black looks: Race and representation*; M. B. Zinn, P. Hondagneu-Sotelo, and M. Messner (1997), *Through the prism of difference: Readings on sex and gender.*

24. B. Friedan (1963), p. 26.

25. J. Allan (1993), "Male elementary school teachers," p. 127.

26. E. Disch (1997), *Reconstructing gender: A multicultural anthology*, p. 1.

27. D. H. J. Morgan (1992); or what Barrie Thorne, in *Gender play*, discusses as "big man bias," pp. 97-99.

28. M. Kimmel (1994), "Masculinity as homophobia."

29. M. Messner (1993), "Changing men and feminist politics in the United States."

30. S. Coltrane (1994), "Theorizing masculinities in contemporary social science"; see especially p. 42 and pp. 55-56.

31. R. Connell (1995), *Masculinities*, p. 90; see also S. Coltrane (1989), "Household labor and the routine production of gender"; J. Applegate and L. W. Kaye (1993), "Male elder care givers."

32. J. Lever, (1978). "Sex differences in the complexity of children's play and games." She points out that boys are allowed to join in girls' games, but must play the "buffoon" in order to escape ridicule. Girls, on the other hand, are expected to join in as serious participants. In *Gender Play*, B. Thorne devotes several pages to the past and present meanings of the label "tomboy" and "sissy." While both connote gender deviance, sissy has "relentlessly negative connotation" and ultimately refers to a "failed male" (pp. 115-116).

33. By "dangerous," I mean several things. Some may suspect that any man who is gay is a pedophile. Others are fearful that his "gayness" can rub off on the children via a type of cultural transmission.

34. C. L. Williams (1993), introduction to *Doing women's work: Men in nontraditional occupations*; D. Buchbinder (1994), *Masculinities and identities.*

35. D. Buchbinder (1994), *Masculinities and identities*, p. 34.

36. H. Becker (1995), *The power of inertia*, p. 306.

37. L. Kramer (1991), "Social class and occupational desegregation"; J. E. Williams & D. L. Best (1990). *Measuring sex stereo-*

types: A multinational study; see also C. Montecinos and L. Nielsen (1997), "Gender and cohort differences in university students' decisions to become elementary teacher education majors." In these works the stereotype that men work for extrinsic rewards and women for intrinsic (widely held in U.S.) is debunked in favor of a more gender neutral perspective that distributes these motivations more evenly across women and men.

38. C. L. Williams (1989), *Gender differences at work: Women and men in nontraditional occupations*. I added the emphasis on "their own" because this is an all-too-common approach in mainstream literature. Men's "decisions" to behave in traditionally masculine ways are presented as individual choices, neglecting societal norms and sanctions that target men.

39. See for example J. Acker (1988), "Class, gender, and the relations of distribution"; J. Gerson & K. Peiss (1985), "Boundaries, negotiations, consciousness: Reconceptualizing gender relations"; L. Kramer (1991), "Social class and occupational desegregation"; R. Pringle (1988), *Secretaries talk*; B. Reskin (1991), "Bring the men back in: Sex differentiation and the devaluation of women's work"; B. Reskin & P. Roos (1990), *Job queues, gender queues*.

40. C. L. Williams (1992), "The glass escalator: Hidden advantages for men in the 'female' professions."

41. B. Berg (1989), *Qualitative research methods for the social sciences*; V. J. Janesick (1994), "The dance of qualitative research design"; D. Silverman (1993), *Interpreting qualitative data*. Member validation occurs when participants in our research see our findings and conclusions and indicate that we have presented their story in much the same way they would have, allowing for differences in language.

42. R. Connell (1992), "A very straight gay: Masculinity, homosexual experience, and the dynamics of gender." When men behave in "feminine" ways, they come under scrutiny, yet the particular social scene in which men operate is so feminized that "masculine" behaviors will also draw attention.

43. M. L. Andersen (1993), "Studying across difference: Race, class, and gender in qualitative methods"; N. Denzin (1992),

Symbolic interactionism and cultural studies; M. Fine (1992), *Disruptive voices: The possibilities of feminist research.* The ways that researchers and participants see both the world and the interview process depend on their own respective sets of lived experiences.

44. A. Lorde (1984), *Sister outsider.*

45. P. McIntosh (1995), "White privilege and male privilege," pp. 79-81.

46. M. Frye (1983), "Oppression." Seemingly small events, such as men holding the door open for women or a single advertisement that objectifies women, may be seen as easily circumnavigated or overcome, but the cumulative effect of countless events can be devastating.

47. W. J. Goode (1992), "Why men resist."

48. M. M. Gergen (1988), "Building a feminist methodology"; A. S. Kasper (1994), "A feminist, qualitative methodology: A study of women with breast cancer." By engaging the participants in the research process as "co-researchers," we empower them to structure the research and to steer the inquiry toward the themes that are important to them rather than to the external researcher.

49. M. Messner (1992), *Power at play*; T. Cohen (1991), "Speaking with men: Application of a feminist methodology to the study of men's lives." Men need to know that it is safe to express their feelings and it is not always possible to create this sense. I try to create this sense of safety by being emotionally expressive myself and by asking men frequently how an experience made them feel.

50. F. Cancian (1986), "The feminization of love." Men have been encouraged to demonstrate their love for others in radically different ways from women's expressions (e.g., by working a second job). Unfortunately, these alternative expressions are seen as inferior when compared to "real" love—women's.

Notes for Chapter Two

1. B. Reskin and P. Roos (1990), *Job queues, gender queues*; C. L. Williams (1989), *Gender differences at work.*

2. H. Bradley (1989), *Men's work, women's work*; R. M. Kanter (1977), *Men and women of the corporation*; B. Reskin and I. Padavic (1994), *Women and men at work*; and C. Williams (1989), *Gender differences at work*.

3. E. Hansot and D. Tyack (1988), "Gender in American public schools: Thinking institutionally." Individuals who are immersed in a social scene, such as an occupation, take the gender arrangements for granted, as "the way things are," and do not perceive their days as being structured around gender "rules."

4. See for example, M. E. Thornton (1999), "Reducing wastage among men student teachers in primary courses: A male club approach." Men teachers are presented as entering the profession later than women and after having less than successful or satisfying careers elsewhere. Their entry into teaching, then, is seen as a kind of resignation to a lesser status rather than an awakening to their real potential.

5. C. J. B. DeCorse and S. P. Vogtle (1997), "In a complex voice: The contradictions of male elementary teachers' career choice and professional identity." As so many researchers do, these authors point to key events in men's lives in which children are encountered and found to be less difficult to handle than had been anticipated.

6. See J. Acker (1988), "Class, gender, and the relations of distribution"; C. Cockburn (1983), *Brothers*; R. M. Kanter (1977), *Men and women of the corporation*; R. Leidner (1991), "Serving hamburgers and selling insurance: Gender, work, and identity in interactive service jobs"; B. Reskin & P. Roos (1990), *Job queues, gender queues*; and C. L. Williams (1989), *Gender differences at work*.

7. R. M. Kanter (1977), *Men and women of the corporation*.

8. W. Moore (1962), *The conduct of the corporation*; C. F. Epstein (1970), *Woman's place: Options and limits in professional careers*. The characteristic in question can be age, race, religion, even dress (e.g., wearing one's culturally traditional garb). Despite one's qualifications or performance, the point of difference becomes the focus of the majority group.

9. R. Connell (1987), *Gender and power*, p. 99; J. Acker (1990), "Hierarchies, jobs, bodies: A theory of gendered organizations." Of

course, the idea that men's responsibilities at home would not "compete" with work obligations is a classic self-fulfilling prophecy.

10. R. Leidner (1991), "Serving hamburgers and selling insurance: Gender, work, and identity in interactive service jobs," p. 154; see also J. Acker (1988), "Class, gender, and the relations of distribution."

11. J. P. Spradley and B. J. Mann (1975), *The cocktail waitress: Woman's work in a man's world*; A. Hochschild (1989), *The second shift*.

12. S. E. Martin (1980), *Breaking and entering: Policewomen on patrol*; P. McIntosh (1995), "White privilege and male privilege"; B. Reskin and I. Padavic (1994), *Women and men at work.*

13. L. Telford (1997), "Selves in bunkers: Organizational consequences of failing to verify alternative masculinities." Men who display themselves in non-traditional ways within organizations find themselves marginalized and suspect.

14. P. Berger and T. Luckmann (1967), *The social construction of reality*; H. Blumer (1969), *Symbolic interactionism: Perspective and method.* Social scenes are sites where social actors create meanings and then use these meanings to establish and maintain roles within the social scene.

15. J. Lorber (1997), "Believing is seeing," p. 20.

16. Ibid., p. 22.

17. L. Telford (1997), "Selves in bunkers: Organizational consequences of failing to verify alternative masculinities." Marginalized workers expend a great deal of energy simply trying to fit with the expectations of those who have power over workers. This makes life less complicated, if more stressful.

18. J. Gerson and K. Peiss (1985), "Boundaries, negotiations, consciousness: Reconceptualizing gender relations," p. 322.

19. C. T. Schreiber (1979), *Changing places: Men and women in transitional occupations*; C. West and D. Zimmerman (1987), "Doing Gender."

20. For discussion of creating sex difference, see H. Hartmann (1981), "The unhappy marriage of Marxism and feminism: Toward a more progressive union," and S. Harding (Ed.). (1987), *Feminism*

and methodology.

21. N. Chodorow (1979), "Mothering, male dominance, and capitalism"; and P. Slater (1976), *The pursuit of loneliness* (Rev. Ed.).

22. B. Reskin and I. Padavic (1994), *Women and men at work*, p. 5.

23. E. Hansot and D. Tyack (1988), "Gender in American public schools: Thinking institutionally"; S. E. Martin (1980), *Breaking and entering: Policewomen on patrol.* Organizations have institutionalized certain practices and ideologies that constrain members into gender-typical niches within the organizations.

24. H. Bradley (1989), Men's work, women's work; H. Bradley (1993), "Across the great divide: The entry of men into 'women's jobs'"; P. England and M. S. Herbert (1993), "The pay of men in 'female' occupations"; R. Pringle (1988), *Secretaries talk*; C. L. Williams (1989 & 1992), *Gender differences at work and "The glass escalator."*

25. U.S. Department of Education (1994); NCES (1996).

26. R. Best (1983), *We've all got scars: What boys and girls learn in school*; C. Steedman (1988), "'The mother-made-conscious': The historical development of a primary school pedagogy." The point being made is that children are nurtured and cared for in the early grades and learning takes place through this care.

27. C. L. Williams (1992), "The glass escalator: Hidden advantages for men in the 'female' professions"; J. Allan (1994), *Anomaly as exemplar: The meanings of role-modeling for men elementary teachers.*

28. J. Allan (1994), *Anomaly as exemplar: The meanings of role-modeling for men elementary teachers*, p. 9.

29. C. L. Williams (1992), "The glass escalator: Hidden advantages for men in the 'female' professions," pp. 257-261.

30. J. Allan (1994), *Anomaly as exemplar: The meanings of role-modeling for men elementary teachers*, p. 4.

31. NCES (1996).

32. J. Pleck (1987), "The theory of male sex-role identity: Its rise and fall, 1936 to the present."

Notes for Chapter Three

1. B. Martin and C. T. Mohanty (1986), "Feminist politics: What's home got to do with it?" By constructing a "home equals safety and outside world equals danger" dichotomy, we effectively deny the dangers of home and the comforts of outside, reinforcing the idea that gender must be thought of in binary terms.

2. B. Reskin (1991), "Bring the men back in: Sex differentiation and the devaluation of women's work." With both men and women performing the same jobs (composed of the same tasks), the tendency to pay the genders unequally will be challenged.

3. C. Skelton (1994), "Sex, males, and young children," p. 90. Also see my Chapter Four.

4. Ibid., p. 91.

5. Ibid., p. 88.

6. Ibid., p. 88; R. Connell (1995), *Masculinities*; see also R. Best (1983), *We've all got scars: What boys and girls learn in school*. Researchers such as Connell and Best speak of the "hidden curriculum" in school. Students learn, for example, to form lines, to sit quietly, and often to divide into groups according to sex. They also learn many of the "appropriate" gender roles that will stay with them for life.

7. B. Reskin (1991), "Bring the men back in: Sex differentiation and the devaluation of women's work"; J. Allan (1993), "Male elementary school teachers: Experiences and perspectives." This mechanism of exclusion does not have to be seen as intentional. Like many instances of discrimination, the act is so embedded (institutionalized) into daily life that it passes as "life as usual."

8. For more information on the stigmatization of homosexuality, see M. Foucault (1978), *The history of sexuality, Vol. 1*; E. K. Sedgewick (1985), *Between men: English literature and male homosocial desire*; and C. Owens (1992), "Outlaws: Gay men in feminism."

9. J. Allan (1994), *Anomaly as exemplar: The meanings of role-modeling for men elementary teachers*.

10. L. Chusmir (1990), "Men who make nontraditional career

choices." The very decision to do work normally associated with women is cause to suspect men's sexuality, motivations, and even moral character.

11. G. Herek (1993), "The context of anti-gay violence: Notes on cultural psychological heterosexism," p. 258.

12. Ibid., p. 92.

13. J. Butler (1990), "Gender trouble, feminist theory and psychoanalytic discourse." In this way, heterosexual men are also constrained by homophobia.

14. R. Connell (1987), *Gender and power*. Connell shows us the ways that a society can place power and more desirable occupations in the hands of men while simultaneously preventing us from fulfilling basic emotional needs.

15. M. Foucault (1978), *The history of sexuality, Vol. 1*; G. Rubin (1984), "Thinking sex: Notes for a radical theory of the politics of sexuality." Since the vast majority of the harm that befalls children comes at the hands of heterosexuals (some of them women), this symbolic use of the homosexual as the epitome of child endangerment is worth extensive critique.

16. J. Allan (1994), *Anomaly as exemplar: The meanings of role-modeling for men elementary teachers*; T. Carrigan, R. Connell, and J. Lee (1987), "Toward a new sociology of masculinity." Homophobia has different implications for men and women. For women, it can be seen as the irrational fear and dislike of homosexuals. For men, it is additionally a fear of being seen as effeminate— a rational fear, since the possibilities of powerful negative sanctions exist in all areas of social life.

17. L. Williams and W. J. Villemez (1993), "Seekers and finders: Male entry and exit in female-dominated jobs."

18. R. Emerson (1983), *Contemporary field studies*; V. Janesick (1994), "The dance of qualitative research design: Metaphor, methodolatry, and meaning."

19. G. Herek (1993), "The context of anti-gay violence: Notes on cultural psychological heterosexism."

20. H. Garfinkel (1967), *Studies in ethnomethodology*. Garfinkel posits that we "know" people through our exposure to

symbolic characterizations of them. Much like stereotypes, these "identikits" serve as categories into which unknown persons can be inserted in order to be placed into our perspective of the world and how it works.

21. C. Wang and D. Daro (1997), *Current trends in child abuse reporting and fatalities: The results of the 1996 annual fifty-state survey*; American Association for Protecting Children (AAPC) (1988), *Highlights of official child neglect and abuse reporting, 1986.* Other forms of maltreatment include physical and verbal abuse, neglect, and abandonment.

22. E. D. Nelson (1994), "Females who sexually abuse children: A discussion of gender stereotypes and symbolic assailants"; H. Garfinkel (1967), Studies in ethnomethodology.

23. R. Schulz (1997), *Interpreting teacher practice: Two continuing stories.*

24. D. S. David and R. Brannon (1976), *The forty-nine percent majority.* In explaining the different forms that masculinity can take, the authors describe various aspects of the "male role" using metaphors such as "sturdy oak," "give 'em hell," "no sissy stuff," and "the big wheel." These represent, respectively, stoicism, violence, an anti-feminine mandate, and the need to be recognized as the best at something, even an activity seen as superfluous.

25. C. West and D. Zimmerman (1987), "Doing gender"; J. Allan (1993), "Male elementary school teachers"; R. Pringle (1993), "Male secretaries"; and C. L. Williams (1992), "The glass escalator: Hidden advantages for men in the 'female' professions."

26. R. M. Kanter (1977), *Men and women of the corporation*; B. Reskin and P. Roos (1990), *Job queues, gender queues.* Most marginalized workers, whatever the mechanism of marginalization may be, report having to maintain higher standards than the majority workers. Majority workers are assumed to be competent unless they make an error, while marginalized are assumed less than competent and continuously must prove their merit.

27. T. J. Gerschick and A. S. Miller (1994), "Gender identities at the crossroads of masculinity and physical disability."

28. R. Pringle (1993), "Male secretaries"; C. L. Williams

(1992), "The glass escalator: Hidden advantages for men in the 'female' professions." Neither author explains why men's self-esteem would suffer, though the implication is that this is self-imposed, which is inconsistent with the men's own narratives and with theories of constructivist sociology.

29. In this number, I have included only those men currently teaching, not those enrolled in teacher education.

30. See T. J. Gerschick and A. S. Miller (1994), "Gender identities at the crossroads of masculinity and physical disability," for a similar discussion of how men with disabilities negotiate a "new" form of masculinity that simply ignores or negates the usual, hegemonic, male attributes.

31. M. Messner (1992), *Power at play*, p. 91; P. Slater (1976), *The pursuit of loneliness*. Both authors describe the way that interpersonal behavior between men tends to be made safe from scrutiny by institutionalized assignment of well-defined limits to closeness (e.g., athletes patting each others' posteriors).

32. As I recounted these and other stories to other faculty, one told me a story of a man who playfully "headbutts" his students as a form of greeting or kudos.

33. R. Pringle (1993), "Male secretaries"; M. Strober and D. Tyack (1980), "Why do women teach and men manage?"; C. L. Williams (1992), "The glass escalator: Hidden advantages for men in the 'female' professions." This "principal-in-training" stereotype is extremely troubling for most of the men I spoke with because it has the effect of trivializing their presence in the elementary school environment. There is also the tendency to dismiss any difficulties the men may be experiencing as temporary and "worth the bother" since they are on their way to bigger and better things in the profession.

34. L. Blum and V. Smith (1988), "Women's mobility in the corporation: A critique of the politics of optimism."

35. R. M. Kanter (1977), *Men and women of the corporation*.

36. N. Noddings (1984), *Caring: A feminine approach to ethics and moral education*.

37. J. Nias (1989), *Primary teachers talking*.

38. B. J. Risman (1987), "Intimate relationships from a micro-

structural perspective: Men who mother," p. 7. The lives of women and men need to be examined in the context of the network of ongoing relationships in which they are immersed on a daily basis.

39. J. King (1995), *Uncommon caring: Learning from men who teach young children.* This idea of "openly" recruiting men (that is, there is much talk of wanting to recruit men) is denied by the clearly hostile attitudes shown toward men who display the very characteristics that make for success in early education.

Notes for Chapter Four

1. National Center for Education Statistics (NCES) (1996), *Schools and staffing in the U.S.: A statistical profile, 1993-94* (NCES 96-124).

2. P. McIntosh (1995), "White privilege and male privilege."

3. J. Acker (1988), "Class, gender, and the relations of distribution"; S. E. Martin (1980), *Breaking and entering: Policewomen on patrol.* Whenever members of an underrepresented group enter an occupation as minority workers, they find that the standards that are in place (both explicit and implicit) have been established to match the attributes of the majority group.

4. National Association of Elementary School Principals (NAESP) (1996), *Principal profile.*

5. C. L. Williams (1992), "The glass escalator: Hidden advantages for men in the 'female' professions," pp. 260-261.

6. This was evident from the first small survey that I performed at the outset of my research.

7. I borrowed this from E. Hansot and D. Tyack (1988), "Gender in American public schools: Thinking institutionally." They remind us to look at the way the organization structures workers' lives in ways to produce gendered work conditions.

8. See for example S. Coltrane (1994), "Theorizing masculinities in contemporary social science"; and T. Laqueur (1992), "The facts of fatherhood."

9. C. L. Williams (1992), "The glass escalator: Hidden advan-

tages for men in the 'female' professions," pp. 257-262.

10. Ibid., p. 262.

11. Ibid., p. 257.

12. J. Allan (1993), "Male elementary school teachers: Experiences and perspectives."

13. C. L. Williams (1992), "The glass escalator: Hidden advantages for men in the 'female' professions," p. 261.

14. National Center for Education Statistics (NCES) (1996), *Schools and staffing in the U.S.: A statistical profile, 1993-94* (NCES 96-124).

15. A. Cognard-Black (1997), "Will they stay or will they go?: Occupational attrition among male elementary school teachers in the United States."

16. National Association of Elementary School Principals (NAESP) (1996), *Principal profile.*

17. T. Cohen (1991), "Speaking with men: Application of a feminist methodology to the study of men's lives"; M. Kaufman (1993), *Cracking the armor: Power and pain in the lives of men*; M. Messner (1987), "The meaning of success," and (1992), *Power at play*. I went into this project determined to pose questions to men that we would typically pose to women—about how they feel, about what they fear, and about what obstacles they face in terms of others' perceptions of them.

18. C. L. Williams (1992), "The glass escalator: Hidden advantages for men in the 'female' professions"; see also J. Allan (1993), "Male elementary school teachers: Experiences and perspectives"; H. Bradley (1993), "Across the great divide: The entry of men into 'women's jobs'"; R. Pringle (1988), *Secretaries talk*; and B. Reskin (1991), "Bring the men back in: Sex differentiation and the devaluation of women's work." While some of these authors do not explicitly say that work conditions do not need changing, most focus their presentations on the men's psychological state, leaving the reader to conclude that it is the men who must change, rather than the institution.

19. C. L. Williams (1992), "The glass escalator: Hidden advantages for men in the 'female' professions," p. 265.

20. J. Allan (1993), "Male elementary school teachers: Experi-

ences and perspectives."

21. This phase of my research is in its beginning stages. Since hearing of the possibility of "tracking" in schools of education, I have set out to interview men in school and accompany them to class.

22. H. L. Freidus (1990), "The call of the sirens: The influence of gender in the decision to choose teaching as a career change." Our society believes teaching is for women and supports girls'/women's entry into the world of children while discouraging, even preventing, the entry of boys/men; then we point to the scarcity of men in children's lives to prove we made the correct decisions all along.

Notes for Chapter Five

1. S. Kessler and W. McKenna (1978), *Gender: An ethnomethodological approach.* The "taken-for-granted" world as we uncritically live it is a major focus of ethnomethodologists.

2. N. Chodorow (1978), *The reproduction of mothering*; and L. Balbus (1982), *Marxism and domination*; D. Dinnerstein (1976), *The mermaid and the minotaur.* Early in life, boys must shift from their mothers to some model of masculinity. Since there is such a drastic shortage of men in the lives of our children, examples of masculinity must be found elsewhere, particularly the popular media, and then shared among peers.

3. R. Best (1983), *We've all got scars: What boys and girls learn in school*; N. Chodorow (1978), *The reproduction of mothering*; D. S. David and R. Brannon (1976), T*he forty-nine percent majority*; P. Garfinkel (1991), "Mentors we never meet: Reflections of men in the media's eye." There is an emphasis on proscriptive (what not to do) rather than prescriptive (what should be done) learning in boys' lives.

4. B. Thorne (1993), *Gender play: What girls and boys learn in school.* Thorne suggests that gender may not always be the most salient organizing principle at work in an individual's life. However, it may be far more salient than the individuals themselves know.

5. For a critique of role theory in gender studies, see T. Carrigan,

R. Connell, and J. Lee (1987), "Toward a new sociology of masculinity" or J. Stacey and B. Thorne (1985), "The missing feminist revolution in sociology."

6. J. Pleck (1987), "The theory of male sex-role identity: Its rise and fall, 1936 to the present."

7. M. Messner (1990), "Men studying masculinity: Some epistemological issues in sport sociology"; B. Thorne (1993), *Gender play: What girls and boys learn in school.*

8. T. Carrigan, R. Connell, and J. Lee (1987), "Toward a new sociology of masculinity."

9. J. Pleck (1987), "The theory of male sex-role identity: Its rise and fall, 1936 to the present," p. 23.

10. H. Brod (1987), The making of masculinities.

11. R. Connell (1993), "The big picture: Masculinities in recent world history."

12. S. Ortner (1974), "Is female to male as nature is to culture." Ortner argues that women are associated with the sphere of nature because of reproductive capacities. This association logically puts men into the cultural sphere (where ideas and material artifacts are produced). These associations are then converted to a division of labor whereby women maintain the domestic world (home and children) and men function in the public sphere of work and politics.

13. T. Parsons and R. Bales (1956), *Family socialization and interaction process.*

14. J. E. Williams and D. L. Best (1990), *Measuring sex stereotypes: A multinational study.*

15. B. Friedan (1981), *The second stage*, p. 125.

16. R. M. Kanter (1977), *Men and women of the corporation.*

17. B. D. Adam (1978), *The survival of domination*, p. 43.

18. R. M. Kanter (1977), *Men and women of the corporation.*

19. C. L. Williams (1989), *Gender differences at work: Women and men in nontraditional occupations*, p. 98, emphasis in original. Again, little is discussed about the activities of the organizational majority or the effects of disparate work rules.

20. C. L. Williams (1989), *Gender differences at work: Women and men in nontraditional occupations*, p. 99.

21. R. M. Kanter (1977), *Men and women of the corporation.*

22. M. Kimmel (1994), "Masculinity as homophobia: Fear, shame, and silence in the construction of gender identity," p. 136.

23. M. Kaufman (1994), "Men, feminism, and men's contradictory experience of power."

24. J. Allan (1993), "Male elementary school teachers: Experiences and perspectives."

25. K. Seifert (1985), "Career experiences of men who teach young children."

26. C. L. Williams (1989), *Gender differences at work: Women and men in nontraditional occupations.*

27. D. Gold and M. Reis (1982), "Male teacher effects on young children: A theoretical and empirical consideration." This debate continues today, with many educators denying that there is the need for more men in teaching specifically to prevent boys from developing weak gender identities.

28. J. Pleck (1987), "The theory of male sex-role identity: Its rise and fall, 1936 to the present."

29. J. Allan (1994), "Anomaly as exemplar: The meanings of role-modeling for men elementary teachers." Allan is critical of the way that some research is presented in that these myths are left to stand without being questioned.

Notes for Chapter Six

1. J. King (1995), *Uncommon caring: Learning from men who teach young children,* p. 35.

2. S. Ortner (1974), "Is female to male as nature is to culture?"

3. A. Minas (1993), *Gender basics.*

4. L. Chusmir (1990), "Men who make nontraditional career choices."

5. M. Kaufman (1987), B*eyond patriarchy: Essays by men on pleasure, power, and change.*

6. A. Hochschild (1983), *The managed heart: Commercialization and human feeling.* Hochschild's point is that there are "emotion

rules" that determine what emotional displays are acceptable for men and women under varying circumstances. Men are restricted to a narrow range of allowable displays when compared to women.

7. J. Cook and M. Fonow (1986), "Knowledge and women's interests: Feminist methodology in the field of sociology."

8. A. Richert (in C. Brody, D. Schroeder, K. Webb, R. Schulz, and A. Richert, Eds., 1994), *Collaborative narrative inquiry: Fidelity and the ethics of caring in teacher research.*

9. C. Z. Enns (1993), "Twenty years of feminist counseling and therapy." By sharing experiences and feelings about events with others, women have created a space within which their unique perspective (compared to the dominant male-centered worldview) can take shape and about which a vocabulary, grounded in real situations, can develop.

10. C. DiStefano (1990), "Dilemmas of difference: Feminism, modernity, and postmodernism." DiStefano argues that women have not yet had their enlightenment. They have not yet influenced the deductive (objective) sciences. I would argue that men have not yet formed a subjective voice that represents our real experiences.

11. M. E. Thornton (1999), "Reducing wastage among men student teachers in primary courses: A male club approach."

12. J. Nelson (1993), *Volunteer slavery: My authentic Negro experience.* As a black woman in white corporate America, Nelson found herself marginalized for both her skin color and her sex. As a member (no matter how marginalized) of corporate America, she was scrutinized by other blacks.

13. R. Hale (1990), "Cultural insensitivity to sexist language toward men"; B. E. Hort, B. I. Fagot, and M D. Leinbach (1990), "Are people's notions of maleness more stereotypically framed than their notions of femaleness?" In an interesting experiment, Hale and colleagues asked participants to judge statements as either "sexist toward men," "sexist toward women," or "neutral." They constructed possibly offensive statements and then presented them to participants after alternatively inserting terms such as "girlfriend," "boyfriend," and "significant other" into the instruments. Participants found allusions to "girlfriends" sexist while those to "significant others" and

"boyfriends" were found neutral despite the content of the statements being identical in every other respect.

14. P. Willis (1977), *Learning to labor: How working class kids get working class jobs*. The students Willis studied worked very hard at separating themselves from the teachers and from serious students. In so doing, they were inadvertently solidifying their own working-class status.

15. J. Nelson (1993), *Volunteer slavery: My authentic Negro experience*.

16. E. Hansot and D. Tyack (1988), "Gender in American public schools: Thinking institutionally."

17. J. Levine (1978), *Who will raise the children?* The problem is that Levine, like others, focuses on the idea that men are producing the barriers in their efforts to be seen as real men. What we need more of is a critique of the construction of the norms that are at the heart of the men's activities and a close look at the sanctions that maintain the norms.

18. C. L. Williams (1989), *Gender differences at work: Women and men in nontraditional occupations*. There are clear and measurable external forces working on boys and men from birth. That we have internalized the expectations of society is not particularly strange. We can find clear evidence that groups internalize others' perceptions of themselves even to their own detriment.

19. D. L. Cohen (1990), "Early childhood educators bemoan the scarcity of males in teaching." Parents' suspicions about men's motivations or qualifications, community members' queries about the reasonableness of putting children at possible risk, and blatantly disparate work rules are surely external to the men. So is the constant threat of criminal action in the case of a slip-up.

20. W. C. Ayers (1986), "The same but different: A male teacher's perspective." The simple accusation of impropriety marks the probable end of a man's career in child care and early education.

21. J. Levine (1978), *Who will raise the children?*

22. T. Laqueur (1992), "The facts of fatherhood."

23. B. Thorne (1993), *Gender play: What girls and boys learn in school*, p. 5.

24. R. M. Kanter (1977), *Men and women of the corporation.* Majority members are more content to have minority members act in stereotypical ways, thus confirming their world view.

25. A. Hochschild (1983), *The managed heart*: Commercialization and human feeling, p. 63.

26. A. Hochschild (1989), *The second shift*, p. 187.

27. M. Messner (1987), "The meaning of success," p. 209.

28. Ibid., p. 187.

29. See for example A. Rich (1980), "Compulsory heterosexuality and lesbian existence"; S. Ruddick (1989), *Maternal thinking: Towards a politics of peace*; L. Segal (1990), *Slow motion: Changing masculinities, changing men.*

30. R. Milkman (1987), *Gender at work: The dynamics of job segregation by sex during World War II*, p. 50. Milkman says that "idioms of sex-typing" are simply applied to whatever jobs the women or men happen to be holding. Some jobs require "scripts" that structure the way we do gender, and some scripts assume that the actors will be of one gender. In this study it was evident that there is an assumption that the teachers and the primary parents will be women.

31. J. Allan (1994), *Anomaly as exemplar: The meanings of role-modeling for men elementary teachers.*

32. E. Hansot and D. Tyack (1988), "Gender in American public schools: Thinking institutionally" p. 742.

33. B. Thorne (1993), *Gender play: What girls and boys learn in school.*

34. D. Wellman (1977), *Portraits of white racism.* Wellman talks about the problem encountered in writing about our findings of others' lives in a way that authentically reflects their perspective yet will be acceptable to the academic community in terms of the format in which we must present our findings.

35. N. Denzin (1970), *The research act: An introduction to sociological methods.*

36. See D. Silverman (1993), Interpreting qualitative data; and V. Janesick (1994), "The dance of qualitative research design: Metaphor, methodolatry, and meaning," for other researchers' views

on presenting emerging findings to participants in order to have them check on the validity of findings.

37. For example J. Allan (1994), *Anomaly as exemplar: The meanings of role-modeling for men elementary teachers*; W. C. Ayers (1986), "The same but different: A male teacher's perspective"; H. L. Freidus (1990), "The call of the sirens: The influence of gender in the decision to choose teaching as a career change"; C. L. Williams (1992), "The glass escalator: Hidden advantages for men in the 'female' professions."

38. J. Flax (1990), "Postmodernism and gender relations in feminist theory." Women as a group are subordinated to men as a group. The basis of their subordination is gender, which is a social construction. A feminist reconstruction begins with the deconstruction of gender as an organizing principle and results in equality between men and women.

39. R. Connell (1993), "The big picture: Masculinities in recent world history," p. 598.

40. H. Brod (1994), "Some thoughts of some histories of some masculinities," p. 91.

41. b. hooks (1992), *Black looks: Race and representation.*

42. P. H. Collins (1991), *Black feminist thought.*

43. N. Hartsock (1987), "The feminist standpoint; B. Reskin (1991), "Bring the men back in: Sex differentiation and the devaluation of women's work." Standpoint, at its heart, is the realization that a group's lived experiences produce a unique perspective on the social world. The more marginalized a group is, the less likely the group will be to have a vested interest in preserving the status quo and the more likely they will be to perceive its weaknesses.

44. N. Hartsock (1987), "The feminist standpoint"; D. Smith (1974), "Women's perspective as a radical critique of sociology." Each new perspective (standpoint) will enrich social science's repertoire of approaches to examining the social world and increase the possibility of understanding the human condition.

45. M. L. Andersen (1993), "Studying across difference: Race, class, and gender in qualitative methods," p. 39.

46. M. Messner (1990), "Men studying masculinity: Some epis-

temological issues in sport sociology," p. 137.

47. Ibid., p. 148.

48. S. Coltrane (1989), "Household labor and the routine pro-duction of gender."

49. R. Connell (1995), *Masculinities*.

50. B. Friedan (1981), *The second stage*.

51. S. E. Martin (1980), *Breaking and entering: Policewomen on patrol*.

52. B. Reskin (1991), "Bring the men back in: Sex differentia-tion and the devaluation of women's work." Reskin argues that it is in the best interest of the corporate capitalist system for women and men to be assigned into different recesses of the work world and for these assignments to have the appearance of being a result of natu-ral differences.

53. C. L. Williams (1992), "The glass escalator: Hidden advan-tages for men in the 'female' professions."

54. J. Allan (1994), *Anomaly as exemplar: The meanings of role-modeling for men elementary teachers*, p. 14.

55. In particular, see B. D. Adam (1978), *The survival of domi-nation*; C. F. Epstein (1970), *Woman's place: Options and limits in professional careers*; and R. M. Kanter (1977), *Men and women of the corporation*.

56. J. Nelson (1993), V*olunteer slavery: My authentic Negro experience*.

57. See J. Nelson (1993), *Volunteer slavery: My authentic Negro experience*; W. B. Swann, B. W. Pelham, and K. S. Krull (1989), "Agreeable fancy or disagreeable truth? How people reconcile their self-enhancement and self-verification needs"; L. Telford (1997), "Selves in bunkers: Organizational consequences of failing to verify alternative masculinities"; H. M. Trice (1993), *Occupa-tional cul-tures in the workplace*. Tokens are likely to confirm the expectations of the majority group that most members of the marginalized group are incapable of performing to the standards of the occupation and that the tokens represent a small segment of the marginalized popu-lation who are unique, exceptional.

58. C. Skelton (1994), "Sex, males, and young children."

59. J. Nelson (1993), *Volunteer slavery: My authentic Negro experience.*

60. J. King (1995), *Uncommon caring: Learning from men who teach young children.*

61. J. Applegate and L. W. Kaye (1993), "Male elder care givers." In general, men are not raised caring for others. The provision of personal care needs to be learned over time, such as through babysitting, or even through the simple act of brushing another's hair.

62. J. Jacobs (1993), "Men in female-dominated fields," p. 52.

63. J. Lever (1978), "Sex differences in the complexity of children's play and games," p. 485. We have finally recognized that girls/women have most likely not lived through the kinds of experiences that boys/men have. Sports, play-fighting, competition, building things, and arithmetic games give men an advantage in the world of work. It is an advantage that is unearned and simply the result of differential socialization. Educational, social, and business organizations are beginning to provide opportunities for girls and women to catch up in terms of becoming comfortable with the concepts and behaviors with which boys and men are more familiar. This same approach is needed to allow men into the world of children.

64. T. Cohen (1990), "Speaking with men: Application of a feminist methodology to the study of men's lives"; and S. Coltrane (1989), "Household labor and the routine production of gender."

65. R. L. Anderson (1991), "No one told me."

Notes for Chapter Seven

1. A. de Saint Exupery (1943/1971), *The Little Prince*, p. 5.

2. M. Weber (1949), *On the methodology of the social sciences.* Verstehen means more than just understanding others' points of view. It more closely resembles "walking in their shoes" and seeing the world the same way they do.

3. J. Spradley (1979), *The ethnographic interview.* The purpose

of the ethnographic interview is to allow the participants to teach us about their lives. They, in effect, structure the interview for us by giving us clues to the important meaning systems that exist for them.

4. A. Oakley (1981), "Interviewing women." Traditional interviews are too researcher-centered. The participants are the real experts on their lives.

5. C. W. Franklin (1984), *The changing definition of masculinity*; and M. Kimmel (1991), "From separate spheres to sexual equality: Men's responses to feminism at the turn of the century" Most research into the lives of men stops at the surface, dwelling on the nature of men's statuses.

6. S. Bell and M. Yalom (1990), *Revealing lives: Autobiography, biography, and gender*.

7. H. Blumer (1969), *Symbolic interactionism: Perspective and method*. A sensitizing concept is any cultural symbol that calls our attention to a distinct social process. Once we become aware of the existence of a process, we are capable of recognizing its presence whenever we encounter it. First, however, we must become aware of it.

8. C. H. Persell (1977), *Education and inequality: A theoretical and empirical synthesis*. Persell presents a very sophisticated model of social class that is multidimensional, including such variables as home ownership, educational strategies for children, occupation, and others. Most of the men come from a middle class background if we apply Persell's model, yet most claim now to be working class.

9. D. Harper (1994), "What problems do you confront?" Harper suggests a simple, yet effective way to launch an ethnographic interview. It takes us into the heart of the informant's daily life and sets the pace as open-ended.

10. M. Q. Patton (1990), *Qualitative evaluation and research methods* (2nd ed.).

11. T. Cohen (1991), "Speaking with men: Application of a feminist methodology to the study of men's lives"; M. Duneier (1992), *Slim's table: Race, respectability and masculinity*; M. Messner (1992), *Power at play*.

12. M. Q. Patton (1990), *Qualitative evaluation and research methods* (2nd ed.).

13. N. Denzin (1989), *Interpretive biography.*

14. R. Traver (1987), "Autobiography, feminism and the study of teaching."

15. E. Mishler (1986), *Research interviewing.* This is also in agreement with the "grounded theory" approach of B. Glaser and A. Strauss (1967), *The discovery of grounded theory.* Both the data and the questions come from the informants' narratives.

16. C. Gilligan (1982), *In a different voice.*

17. C. Briggs (1986), *Learning to ask: A sociolinguistic appraisal of the role of the interview in social science research.*

18. M. Miles and M. Huberman (1984), *Qualitative data analysis*, p. 58. These themes are meant to initiate an exploration into the data collected. They act as a temporary frame to begin building a taxonomy of meaning. The initial taxonomy begins transforming in response to the addition of new data almost immediately.

19. J. Spradley (1979), *The ethnographic interview.* Spradley takes his students though the collection, analysis, and presentation of research findings by using a series of steps that takes the student deeper into the meaning system of the informants.

20. B. Glaser and A. Strauss (1967), *The discovery of grounded theory: Strategies for qualitative research.*

21. Ibid., p. 101.

22. C. Briggs (1986), *Learning to ask: A sociolinguistic appraisal of the role of the interview in social science research.* When we impose our meanings and form of dialogue on others, the resulting data are, potentially, as much an artifact of our perspective as of our informants'.

23. Ibid., p. 90.

24. R. A. Krueger (1988), *Focus group: A practical guide for applied research.*

25. D. L. Morgan and M. Spanish (1984), "Focus groups: A new tool for qualitative research."

26. H. S. Becker and B. Geer (1960), "Participant observation: The analysis of qualitative field data."

27. D. Wellman (1977), *Portraits of white racism*, pp. 53-56.

28. R. Emerson (1983), *Contemporary field studies*; S. Reinharz (1992), *Feminist methods in social science*. Reflection is necessary to determine how much of the emerging picture is attributable to the researcher's definition of the situation and how much is truly a reflection of the participants' perspective. It is very easy to impose meaning where it does not exist.

29. H. Brod (1987), *The making of masculinities: The new men's studies*.

30. D. Buchbinder (1994), *Masculinities and identities*.

31. A. K. Daniels (1983), "Self-disclosure and self-discovery in fieldwork," p. 206.

32. D. Buchbinder (1994), *Masculinities and identities*, p. 6.

33. R. Connell (1985), "Theorizing gender," p. 336.

34. C. Geertz (1988), *Works and lives: The anthropologist as author*, p. 76.

35. N. Noddings (1984), *Caring: A feminine approach to ethics and moral education*.

36. D. Smith (1974), "Women's perspective as a radical critique of sociology." I was careful, in other words, not to use my position as social scientist to impose a preconceived meaning on their words.

37. R. Coles (1971), *Children of crisis, Vol. 2: Migrants, sharecroppers, and mountaineers*.

References

Acker, J. (1988). Class, gender, and the relations of distribution. *Signs, 13*, 4 73-97.

Acker, J. (1990). Hierarchies, jobs, bodies: A theory of gendered organizations. *Gender and Society, 4*, 139-158.

Adam, B. D. (1978). *The survival of domination.* New York: Elsevier.

Allan, J. (1993). Male elementary school teachers: Experiences and perspectives. In C. Williams (Ed.), *Doing women's work: Men in nontraditional occupations* (pp. 113-127). Newbury Park, CA: Sage.

Allan, J. (1994). *Anomaly as exemplar: The meanings of role-modeling for men elementary teachers.* Dubuque, IA: Tri-College Department of Education (Eric Document Reproduction Service No. ED 378 190).

American Association for Protecting Children (AAPC). (1988). *Highlights of official child neglect and abuse reporting, 1986.* Denver, CO: American Humane Association.

Andersen, M. L. (1993). Studying across difference: Race, class, and gender in qualitative methods. In M. B. Zinn, P. Hondagneu-Sotelo, & M. Messner (Eds.), *Through the prism of difference: Readings on sex and gender* (pp. 70-85). Boston: Allyn and Bacon.

Anderson, R. L. (1991). No one told me. In Y. Ornstein (Ed.), *From the hearts of men* (pp. 60-61). New York: Fawcett.

Applegate, J., & Kaye L. W. (1993). Male elder care givers. In C. L. Williams (Ed.), *Doing women's work: Men in nontraditional occupations* (pp. 152-167). Newbury Park, CA: Sage.

Ayers, W. C. (1986). The same but different: A male teacher's perspective. *Daycare and Early Education, 14,* 24-25.

Balbus, L. (1982). *Marxism and domination.* Princeton: Princeton University Press.

Becker, H. (1995). The power of inertia. *Qualitative Sociology, 18,* 301-309.

Becker, H. S., & Geer, B. (1960). Participant observation: The analysis of qualitative field data. In R. N. Adams & J. J. Preiss (Eds.) *Human organization research* (pp. 267-288). Homewood, IL: Dorsey Press.

Bell, S. G., & Yalom, M. (1990). Introduction. In S. G. Bell & M. Yalom (Eds.), *Revealing lives: Autobiography, biography, and gender* (pp. 1-11). Albany: SUNY Press.

Berg, B. (1989). *Qualitative research methods for the social sciences.* Boston: Allyn & Bacon.

Berger, P., & Luckmann, T. (1967). *The social construction of reality.* New York: Doubleday.

Best, R. (1983). *We've all got scars: What boys and girls learn in school.* Bloomington: Indiana University Press.

Blum, L., & Smith, V. (1988). Women's mobility in the corporation: A critique of the politics of optimism. *Signs, 13,* 528-545.

Blumer, H. (1969). *Symbolic interactionism: Perspective and method.* Englewood Cliffs, NJ: Prentice Hall.

Bradley, H. (1989). *Men's work, women's work.* Cambridge: Polity Press.

Bradley, H. (1993). Across the great divide: The entry of men into "women's jobs." In C. L. Williams (Ed.), *Doing women's work: Men in nontraditional occupations* (pp. 10-27). Newbury Park, CA: Sage.

Briggs, C. (1986). *Learning to ask: A sociolinguistic appraisal of the role of the interview in social science research.* Cambridge: Cambridge University Press.

Brod, H. (Ed.). (1987). *The making of masculinities: The new men's studies*. Boston: Allen & Unwin.

Brod, H. (1994). Some thoughts of some histories of some masculinities. In H. Brod & M. Kaufman (Eds.), *Theorizing masculinities* (pp. 82-96). Newbury Park, CA: Sage.

Brody, C., Schroeder, D., Webb, K., Schulz, R., & Richert, A. (1994). *Collaborative narrative inquiry: Fidelity and the ethics of caring in teacher research*. Paper presented at the annual meeting of the American Educational Research Association (April). New Orleans, LA.

Buchbinder, D. (1994). *Masculinities and identities*. Carlton, Victoria: Melbourne University Press.

Butler, J. (1990). Gender trouble, feminist theory and psychoanalytic discourse. In L. Nicholson (Ed), *Feminism/postmodernism* (pp. 324-340). New York: Routledge.

Cancian, F. (1986). The feminization of love. *Signs, 11*, 692-709.

Carrigan, T., Connell, R. L., & Lee, J. (1987). Toward a new sociology of masculinity. *Theory and Society, 45(5)*, 551-603.

Chodorow, N. (1978). *The reproduction of mothering*. Berkeley: University of California Press.

Chodorow, N. (1979). Mothering, male dominance, and capitalism. In Z. Eisenstein (Ed.), *Capitalist patriarchy and the case for socialist feminism* (pp. 83-106). New York: Monthly Review.

Chusmir, L. (1990). Men who make nontraditional career choices. *Journal of Counseling and Development, 69*, 11-16.

Cockburn, C. (1983). *Brothers*. London: Pluto.

Cognard-Black, A. (1997). *Will they stay or will they go?: Occupational attrition among male elementary school teachers in the United States*. Paper presented at the meeting of the American Sociological Association, Washington, DC.

Cohen, D. L. (1990, October 3). Early childhood educators bemoan the scarcity of males in teaching. *Education Week*, 12-13.

Cohen, T. (1991). Speaking with men: Application of a feminist methodology to the study of men's lives. *Men's Studies Review, 8*, 9-13.

Coles, R. (1971). *Children of crisis, Vol. 2: Migrants, sharecroppers, and mountaineers*. Boston: Little, Brown.

Collins, P. H. (1991). *Black feminist thought*. New York: Routledge.

Coltrane, S. (1989). Household labor and the routine production of gender. *Social Problems, 36*, 473-490.

Coltrane, S. (1994). Theorizing masculinities in contemporary social science. In H. Brod & M. Kaufman (Eds.), *Theorizing masculinities* (pp. 39-60). Thousand Oaks, CA: Sage.

Connell, R. (1985). Theorizing gender. *Sociology, 19*, 330-344.

Connell, R. (1987). *Gender and power*. Stanford, CA: Stanford University Press.

Connell, R. (1992). A very straight gay: Masculinity, homosexual experience, and the dynamics of gender. *American Sociological Review, 57*, 735-751.

Connell, R. (1993). The big picture: Masculinities in recent world history. *Theory and Society, 22*, 597-623.

Connell, R. (1995). *Masculinities*. Berkeley: University of California Press.

Cook, J., & Fonow, M. (1986). Knowledge and women's interests: Feminist methodology in the field of sociology. *Sociological Inquiry, 56*, 2-29.

Daniels, A. K. (1983). Self-disclosure and self-discovery in fieldwork. *Qualitative Sociology, 6*, 195-214.

David, D., & Brannon, R. (Eds.). (1976). *The forty-nine percent majority*. New York: Addison-Wesley.

DeCorse, C. J. B., & Vogtle, S. P. (1997). In a complex voice: The contradictions of male elementary teachers' career choice and professional identity. *Journal of Teacher Education, 48(1)*, 37-46.

Denzin, N. (1970). *The research act: An introduction to sociological methods*. New York: McGraw-Hill.

Denzin, N. (1989). *Interpretive biography*. Newbury Park, CA: Sage.

Denzin, N. (1992). *Symbolic interactionism and cultural studies*. Cambridge, UK: Basil Blackwell.

Dinnerstein, D. (1976). *The mermaid and the minotaur*. New York: Harper Row.

Disch, E. (1997). General introduction. In E. Disch (Ed.), *Reconstructing gender: A multicultural anthology* (pp. 1-18). London: Mayfield.

DiStefano, C. (1990). Dilemmas of difference: Feminism, modernity, and postmodernism. In L. Nicholson (Ed.), *Feminism/ postmodernism* (pp. 63-82). New York: Routledge.

Duneier, M. (1992). *Slim's table: Race, respectability and masculinity*. Chicago: University of Chicago Press.

Emerson, R. (1983). Introduction. In R. Emerson (Ed.), *Contemporary field studies* (pp. 1-35). Prospect Heights, IL: Waveland Press.

England, P., & Herbert, M. S. (1993). The pay of men in "female" occupations. In C. L. Williams (Ed.), *Doing women's work: Men in nontraditional occupations* (pp. 28-48). Newbury Park, CA: Sage.

Enns, C. Z. (1993). Twenty years of feminist counseling and therapy. *The Counseling Psychologist, 21*, 3-87.

Epstein, C. F. (1970). *Woman's place: Options and limits in professional careers*. Berkeley: University of California Press.

Epstein, C. F. (1991). It's all in the mind: Personality and social structure. In L. Kramer (Ed.), *The sociology of gender* (pp. 84-104). New York: St. Martin's Press.

Fine, M. (1992). *Disruptive voices: The possibilities of feminist research*. Ann Arbor: The University of Michigan Press.

Finkelhor, D., & Williams, L. (1988). *Nursery crimes: Sexual abuse in day care*. Newbury Park, CA: Sage.

Flax, J. (1990). Postmodernism and gender relations in feminist theory. In L. Nicholson (Ed.), *Feminism/postmodernism* (pp. 39-62). New York: Routledge.

Foucault, M. (1978). *The history of sexuality, Vol. 1*. New York: Random House.

Franklin, C. W. (1984). *The changing definition of masculinity*. New York: Plenum Press.

Freidus, H. L. (1990). *The call of the sirens: The influence of gender in the decision to choose teaching as a career change*. (Eric Document Reproduction Service No. ED 322122).

Friedan, B. (1963). *The feminine mystique*. New York: Dell.

Friedan, B. (1981). *The second stage*. New York: Simon and Schuster.

Frye, M. (1983). *The politics of reality*. New York: The Crossing Press.

Garfinkel, H. (1967). *Studies in ethnomethodology*. London: Polity Press.

Garfinkel, P. (1991). Mentors we never meet: Reflections of men in the media's eye. In L. Kramer (Ed.), *The sociology of gender* (pp. 30-41). New York: St. Martin's Press.

Geertz, C. (1988). *Works and lives: The anthropologist as author*. Stanford, CA: Stanford University Press.

Gergen, M. M. (1988). Building a feminist methodology. *Contemporary Social Psychology, 13*, 47-93.

Gerschick, T. J., &. Miller, A. S. (1994). *Gender identities at the crossroads of masculinity and physical disability*. Masculinities, 2,3 4-55.

Gerson, J., & Peiss, K. (1985). Boundaries, negotiations, consciousness: Reconceptualizing gender relations. *Social Problems, 32*, 317-331.

Gilligan, C. (1982). *In a different voice*. Cambridge: Harvard University Press.

Glaser, B., & Strauss, A. (1967). *The discovery of grounded theory: Strategies for qualitative research*. New York: Aldine De Gruyter.

Gold, D., & Reis, M. (1982). Male teacher effects on young children: A theoretical and empirical consideration. *Sex Roles, 8*, 493-513.

Goode, W. J. (1992). Why men resist. In B. Thorne & M. Yalom (Eds.), *Rethinking the family: Some feminist questions* (pp. 287-310). Boston: Northeastern University Press.

Hale, R. (1990). Cultural insensitivity to sexist language toward men. *Journal of Social Psychology, 130*, 697-698.

Hansot, E., & Tyack, D. (1988). Gender in American public schools: Thinking institutionally. *Signs, 13*, 741-760.

Harding, S. (1987). *Feminism and methodology*. Bloomington:

Indiana University Press.

Harper, D. (1994). What problems do you confront? *Qualitative Sociology, 17*, 89-95.

Harrington, M. (1995). *Women lawyers: Rewriting the rules.* New York: Penguin.

Hartmann, H. (1981). The unhappy marriage of Marxism and feminism: Toward a more progressive union. In L. Sargent (Ed.), *Women and revolution: A discussion of the unhappy marriage of Marxism and feminism* (pp. 1-42). London: Pluto Press.

Hartsock, N. (1987). The feminist standpoint. In S. Harding (Ed.), *Feminism and methodology* (pp.157-180). Bloomington: Indiana University Press.

Hearn, J. (1992). The personal, the political, the theoretical. In D. Porter (Ed.), *Between men and feminism*, (pp. 161-181). London: Routledge.

Herek, G. (1993). The context of anti-gay violence: Notes on cultural psychological heterosexism. In L. D. Garnets & D. C. Kimmel (Eds.), *Psychological perspectives on lesbian and gay male experiences* (pp. 254-266). New York: Columbia University Press.

Hochschild, A. (1983). *The managed heart: Commercialization and human feeling.* Berkeley: University of California Press.

Hochschild, A. (1989). *The second shift.* New York: Avon Books.

hooks, b. (1992). *Black looks: Race and representation.* Boston: South End Press.

Hort, B. E., Fagot, B. I., & Leinbach, M. D. (1990). Are people's notions of maleness more stereotypically framed then their notions of femaleness? *Sex Roles, 23*, 1-18.

Jacobs, J. (1993). Men in female-dominated fields. In C. L. Williams (Ed.), *Doing women's work: Men in nontraditional occupations* (pp. 49-63). Newbury Park, CA: Sage.

Janesick, V. J. (1994). The dance of qualitative research design: Metaphor, methodolatry, and meaning. In N. K. Denzin & Y. S. Lincoln (Eds.), *Handbook of qualitative research design* (pp. 209-219). London: Sage.

Jurik, N. (1985). An officer and a lady: Organizational barriers to women working as correctional officers in men's prisons. *Social Problems, 32*, 373-388

Kanter, R. M. (1977). *Men and women of the corporation.* New York: Basic Books.

Kasper, A. S. (1994). A feminist, qualitative methodology: A study of women with breast cancer. *Qualitative Sociology, 17*, 263-281.

Kaufman, M. (Ed.). (1987). *Beyond patriarchy: Essays by men on pleasure, power, and change.* New York: Oxford University Press.

Kaufman, M. (1993). *Cracking the armor: Power and pain in the lives of men.* Toronto: Viking Canada.

Kaufman, M. (1994). Men, feminism, and men's contradictory experience of power. In H. Brod and M. Kaufman (Eds.), *Theorizing masculinities* (pp. 142-164). Thousand Oaks, CA: Sage.

Kessler, S., & McKenna, W. (1978). *Gender: An ethnomethodological approach.* New York: John Wiley & Sons.

Kimmel, M. (1991). From separate spheres to sexual equality: Men's responses to feminism at the turn of the century. In L. Kramer (Ed.), *The sociology of gender* (pp. 301-322). New York: St. Martin's Press.

Kimmel, M. (1994). Masculinity as homophobia: Fear, shame, and silence in the construction of gender identity. In H. Brod and M. Kaufman (Eds.), *Theorizing masculinities* (pp. 119-141). Thousand Oaks, CA: Sage.

Kimmel, M., & Messner, M. 1998. Introduction. In M. Kimmel and M. Messner (Eds.), *Men's lives* (4th ed., pp. 1-3). Boston: Allyn and Bacon.

King, J. (1995). *Uncommon caring: Learning from men who teach young children.* New York: Teachers College Press.

Kramer, L. (1991). Social class and occupational desegregation. In L. Kramer (Ed.), *The sociology of gender* (pp. 288-303). New York: St. Martin's Press.

Krueger, R. A. (1988). *Focus group: A practical guide for applied research.* Newbury Park, CA: Sage.

Laqueur, T. (1992). The facts of fatherhood. In B. Thorne & M.

Yalom (Eds.), *Rethinking the family* (pp. 155-175). Boston: Northeastern University.

Leidner, R. (1995). Serving hamburgers and selling insurance: Gender, work, and identity in interactive service jobs. *Gender and Society, 2*, 154-177.

Lever, J. (1978). Sex differences in the complexity of children's play and games. *American Sociological Review, 43*, 471-483.

Levine, J. A. (1978). *Who will raise the children?* New York: Lippincott.

Lorber, J. (1986). Dismantling Noah's ark. *Sex Roles, 14*, 567-580.

Lorber, J. (1997). Believing is seeing: Biology as ideology. In M. B. Zinn, P. Hondagneu-Sotelo & M. Messner (Eds.), *Through the prism of difference: Readings on sex and gender* (pp. 13-22). Boston: Allyn and Bacon.

Lorde, A. (1984). *Sister outsider*. New York: The Crossing Press.

Martin, B., & Mohanty, C. T. 1986. Feminist politics: What's home got to do with it? In T. DeLauretis (Ed.), *Feminist studies/critical studies* (pp. 191-212). Bloomington: Indiana University Press.

Martin, S. E. (1980). *Breaking and entering: Policewomen on patrol*. Berkeley: University of California Press.

McIntosh, P. (1995). White privilege and male privilege. In M. Andersen & P. H. Collins (Eds.), *Race, class, and gender* (2nd ed., pp. 76-86). New York: Wadsworth.

Messner, M. (1987). The meaning of success. In H. Brod (Ed.), *The making of masculinities* (pp. 193-210). Boston: Allen and Unwin.

Messner, M. (1990). Men studying masculinity: Some epistemological issues in sport sociology. *Sociology of Sport Journal, 7*, 136-153.

Messner, M. (1992). *Power at play*. Boston: Beacon.

Messner, M. (1993). Changing men and feminist politics in the United States. *Theory and Society, 22*, 723-727.

Miles, M., & Huberman, M. (1984). *Qualitative data analysis*. Beverly Hills, CA: Sage.

Milkman, R. (1987). *Gender at work: The dynamics of job segrega-*

tion by sex during World War II. Urbana: University of Illinois Press.

Mills, C. W. (1961). *The sociological imagination*. London: Oxford University Press.

Minas, A. (1993). Introduction. In A. Minas (Ed.), *Gender basics* (pp. 1-8). Belmont, CA: Wadsworth.

Mishler, E. (1986). *Research interviewing*. Cambridge, MA: Harvard University Press.

Montecinos, C., & Nielsen, L. (1997). Gender and cohort differences in university students' decisions to become elementary teacher education majors. *Journal of Teacher Education, 48*, 47-54.

Moore, W. (1962). *The conduct of the corporation*. New York: Random House Vintage.

Morgan, D. H. J. (1981). Men, masculinity and the process of sociological enquiry. In H. Roberts (Ed.), *Doing feminist research* (pp. 83-113). London: Routledge and Kegan Paul.

Morgan, D. H. J. (1992). Discovering men. London: Routledge.

Morgan, D. L., & Spanish, M. (1984). Focus groups: A new tool for qualitative research. *Qualitative Sociology, 7*, 253-270.

Morrison, A., White, R., & Van Velsor, E. (1987). *Breaking the glass ceiling: Can women reach the top of America's largest corporations?* Reading, MA: Addison-Wesley.

National Association of Elementary School Principals (NAESP). (1996). *Principal profile*. Alexandria, VA: National Association of Elementary School Principals.

National Center for Education Statistics (NCES). (1996). *Schools and staffing in the U.S.: A statistical profile, 1993-94* (NCES 96-124). Washington, DC: National Education Data Resource Center.

Nelson, E. D. (1994). Females who sexually abuse children: A discussion of gender stereotypes and symbolic assailants. *Qualitative Sociology, 17*, 63-88.

Nelson, J. (1993). *Volunteer slavery: My authentic Negro experience*. New York: Penguin Books.

Nias, J. (1989). *Primary teachers talking*. New York: Routledge.

Noddings, N. (1984). *Caring: A feminine approach to ethics and moral education*. Berkeley: University of California Press.

Oakley, A. (1981). *Interviewing women*. In H. Roberts (Ed.), Doing feminist research (pp. 30-61). Boston: Routledge and Kegan Paul.

Ortner, S. (1974). Is female to male as nature is to culture? In M. Z. Rosaldo & L. Lamphere (Eds.), *Woman, Culture, and Society* (pp. 67-88). Stanford, CA: Stanford University Press.

Owens, C. (1992). Outlaws: Gay men in feminism. In S. Bryson et al. (Eds.), *Beyond recognition: representation, power, and culture* (pp. 63-91). Berkeley, CA: University of California Press.

Parsons, T., & Bales, R. (1956). *Family socialization and interaction process*. London: Routledge and Kegan Paul.

Patton, M. Q. (1990). *Qualitative evaluation and research methods* (2nd ed.). Newbury Park, CA: Sage.

Persell, C. H. (1977). *Education and inequality: A theoretical and empirical synthesis*. New York: Free Press.

Pleck, J. (1987). The theory of male sex-role identity: Its rise and fall, 1936 to the present. In H. Brod (Ed.), *The making of masculinities: The new men's studies* (pp. 21-38). Boston: Allen & Unwin.

Pringle, R. (1988). *Secretaries talk*. London: Verso.

Pringle, R. (1993). Male secretaries. In C. L. Williams (Ed.), *Doing women's work: Men in nontraditional occupations* (pp. 128-151). Newbury Park, CA: Sage.

Reinharz, S. (1992). *Feminist methods in social science*. New York: Oxford University Press.

Reskin, B. (1991). Bring the men back in: Sex differentiation and the devaluation of women's work. In J. Lorber & S. Farrell (Eds.), *The social construction of gender* (pp. 141-161). Beverly Hills, CA: Sage.

Reskin, B., & Padavic, I. (1994). *Women and men at work*. Thousand Oaks, CA: Pine Forge Press.

Reskin, B., & Roos, P. (1990). *Job queues, gender queues: Explaining women's inroads into male occupations*. Philadelphia: Temple University Press.

Rich, A. (1980). Compulsory heterosexuality and lesbian existence. *Signs, 5*, 631-60.

Risman, B. J. (1987). Intimate relationships from a microstructural perspective: Men who mother. *Gender and Society, 1*, 6-32.

Robinson, C. E. (Ed.). (1976). *Mary Shelley: Collected tales and stories*. Baltimore: Johns Hopkins Press.

Rubin, G. (1975). The traffic in women: Notes on the political economy of sex. In R. Reiter (Ed.), *Toward an anthropology of women* (pp. 157-211). New York: Monthly Review Press.

Rubin, G. (1984). Thinking sex: Notes for a radical theory of the politics of sexuality. In C. Vance (Ed.), *Pleasure and danger* (pp. 267-279). New York: Routledge.

Ruddick, S. (1989). *Maternal thinking: Towards a politics of peace*. Boston: Beacon Press.

Saint Exupery, A. de. (1971). *The little prince*. New York: Harcourt, Brace, Jovanovich. (Original work published 1943)

Schreiber, C. T. (1979). *Changing places: Men and women in transitional occupations*. Cambridge: The MIT Press.

Schulz, R. (1997). *Interpreting teacher practice: Two continuing stories*. New York: Teachers College Press.

Schutz, A. (1970). *On phenomenology and social relations*. Chicago: University of Chicago Press.

Sedgewick, E. K. (1985). *Between men: English literature and male homosocial desire*. New York: Columbia University Press.

Segal, L. (1990). *Slow motion: changing masculinities, changing men*. New Brunswick, NJ: Rutgers University Press.

Seifert, K. (1985). Career experiences of men who teach young children. *The Canadian Journal of Research in Early Childhood Education, 1*, 56-66.

Silverman, D. (1993). *Interpreting qualitative data*. London: Sage.

Shelley, M. W. (1963). *Frankenstein*. London: Dent. (Original work published 1818)

Skelton, C. (1994). Sex, males, and young children. *Gender and Education, 6*, 87-93.

Slater, P. (1976). *The pursuit of loneliness* (Rev. Ed.). Boston: Beacon Books.

Smith, D. (1974). Women's perspective as a radical critique of sociology. *Sociological Inquiry, 44*, 7-13.

Spradley, J. (1979). *The ethnographic interview*. New York: Harcourt Brace Jovanovich.

Spradley, J. (1980). *Participant observation*. New York: Harcourt Brace Jovanovich.

Spradley, J. P., & Mann, B. J. (1975). *The cocktail waitress: Woman's work in a man's world*. New York: Wiley.

Stacey, J., & Thorne, B. (1985). The missing feminist revolution in sociology. *Social Problems, 32(4)*, 301- 316.

Strober, M., & Tyack, D. (1980). Why do women teach and men manage? *Signs, 5*, 494-503.

Swann, W. B., Jr., Pelham, B. W., & Krull, K. S. (1989). Agreeable fancy or disagreeable truth? How people reconcile their self-enhancement and self-verification needs. *Journal of Personality and Social Psychology, 57*, 782-791.

Telford, L. (1997). Selves in bunkers: Organizational consequences of failing to verify alternative masculinities. In Cliff Cheng (Ed.), *Masculinities in organizations* (pp. 130-159). Thousand Oaks, CA: Sage.

Thomas, W. I., &. Thomas, D. S. (1929). *The child in America*. New York: Alfred A. Knopf.

Thorne, B. (1993). *Gender play: What girls and boys learn in school*. New Jersey: Rutgers University Press.

Thornton, M. E. (1999). Reducing wastage among men student teachers in primary courses: A male club approach. *Journal of Education for Teaching, 25*, 41-53.

Traver, R. (1987). Autobiography, feminism and the study of teaching. *Teachers College Record, 88*, 444-452.

Trice, H. M. (1993). *Occupational cultures in the workplace*. Ithaca, NY: ILR.

U.S. Department of Education, Center for Education Statistics. (1994). *Schools and staffing survey, 1990-1991 [United States]: Teacher follow-up survey, 1991-1992*. Washington, DC: U.S. Department of Commerce, Bureau of the Census.

Vetter, B. M. (1981). Women scientists and engineers: Trends in participation. *Science, 214*, 1313-1321.

Wang, C., & Daro, D. (1997). *Current trends in child abuse reporting and fatalities: The results of the 1996 annual fifty-state survey*. Chicago, IL: National Committee to Prevent Child Abuse.

Weber. M. (1949). *On the methodology of the social sciences* (Edited & translated by E. Shils & H. Finch). Glencoe, IL: Free Press.

Wellman, D. (1977). *Portraits of white racism*. London: Cambridge University Press.

West, C., & Zimmerman, D. (1987). Doing gender. *Gender and Society, 1*, 125-151.

Whyte, W. F. (1981). *Street corner society* (3rd Ed.). Chicago: University of Chicago Press.

Williams, C. L. (1989). *Gender differences at work: Women and men in nontraditional occupations*. Berkeley, CA: University of California Press.

Williams, C. L. (1992). The glass escalator: Hidden advantages for men in the "female" professions. *Social Problems, 39*, 253-267.

Williams, C. L. (1993). Introduction. In C. L. Williams (Ed.), *Doing women's work: Men in nontraditional occupations* (pp. 1-9.). Newbury Park, CA: Sage.

Williams, J. E., & Best, D. L. (1990). *Measuring sex stereotypes: A multinational study*. Newbury Park, CA: Sage.

Williams, L., & Villamez, W. J. (1993). Seekers and finders: Male entry and exit in female-dominated jobs. In C. L. Williams (Ed.), *Doing women's work: Men in nontraditional occupations* (pp. 64-90). Newbury Park, CA: Sage.

Willis, P. (1977). *Learning to labor: How working class kids get working class jobs*. New York: Columbia University Press.

Wollstonecraft, M. (1983). *A vindication of the rights of woman*. London: Penguin Classics.

Zinn, M. B., Hondagneu-Sotelo, P., & Messner, M. (1997). Introduction. In M. B. Zinn, P. Hondagneu-Sotelo, & M. Messner (Eds.), *Through the prism of difference: Readings on sex and gender* (pp. 1-8). Boston: Allyn and Bacon.

Name and Subject Index

About the Author

.

After twelve years as a paramedic, Paul Sargent earned his Ph.D. at the University of Southern California, Department of Sociology and Program for the Study of Gender. He is an assistant professor in the sociology department at San Diego State University where he teaches courses in Gender Roles and Qualitative Research Methods. He is continuing his research focus by interviewing men who are enrolled in teacher certificate programs. He is also a member of a team of San Diego State University faculty commissioned to produce a documentary video promoting community service learning in California universities. Since service learning places college students into community agencies such as day care and elementary schools, he hopes to use this video to help counter the myth that childcare and education are exclusively "women's work." Sargent lives in Carlsbad California with Martha Speck, his wife and partner of twenty-five years.